Luke's Case for Christianity

By the same author

Meet Saint Paul

Luke's Case
for
Christianity

R. E. O. WHITE

MOREHOUSE PUBLISHING
Harrisburg, PA • Wilton, CT

© BRF 1987

First published in Great Britain by The Bible Reading Fellowship, Warwick House, 25 Buckingham Palace Road, London SW1W 0PP

American edition published by Morehouse Publishing.
Editorial Office: 78 Danbury Road, Wilton, CT 06897
Corporate Office: P.O. Box 1321, Harrisburg, PA 17105

Library of Congress Cataloging-in-Publication Data

White, R. E. O. (Reginald Ernest Oscar), 1914–
    Luke's case for christianity/R.E.O. White.
        p.   cm.
    Reprint. Originally published : London : Bible Reading Fellowship, 1987.
    ISBN 0-8192-1531-7
    1. Bible. N.T. Luke—Theology.   2. Apologetics—Early church, ca. 30-600.   I. Title.
    BS2595.5.W49   1987
    226.4'06—dc20

Printed by Bocardo Press Ltd, Didcot, England.

CONTENTS

CHAPTER I

The Man Who Wasn't There

All our Gospels are, strictly speaking, anonymous. Authors' names do not appear within the books, but became attached to them in early Christian tradition on grounds which vary in reliability. To understand *Matthew, Mark,* and *John,* knowledge of the actual writer is not of first importance. With *Luke* it is all-important, for the writer's background and experience explain his standpoint and illumine his purpose.

The first step towards identifying the author of the Gospel is to recall that *Luke* and *Acts* are from the same pen, and dedicated to the same person, Theophilus, as the opening words of each book show. Even without this evidence, the close similarity of the two books, in language, style, interests, outlook and purpose, would have led to the same conclusion. Some have pointed to the detailed parallel between the experience of Jesus before the Jewish Sanhedrin (in the Gospel) and that of Paul (in *Acts*) as a deliberate comparison designed by the one author; both were struck upon the mouth, both accused of treason, both delivered by the Jews to the Romans, and both repeatedly declared innocent. Others find a similar correspondence between the death of Jesus and that of Stephen (compare Acts 7:57–60 with Luke 23:18, 34, 46).

That whoever wrote *Acts* also wrote the Gospel has indeed rarely been questioned, and never upon serious grounds. The summary account of Christ's ascension in the Gospel, and the fuller account in *Acts*, are admittedly different, but not conflicting. The tradition of the church has simply accepted that the books had one author, and proceeded to draw certain conclusions.

A Companion of Paul

For the writer of *Acts* was, in all probability, a travelling companion of Paul, present with him and Silas at Philippi, and again on the journey from Philippi to Jerusalem via Cyprus and Caesarea. He apparently stayed with Paul at Jerusalem, travelled with him back to Caesarea, and two years later on to Rome, via Malta. We might have assumed this from the detailed knowledge which the writer reveals, of letters, speeches, conversations, persons, places, and the storm at sea. But the occurrence of 'we' or 'us' in

Acts 16:10–17 (nine times), 20:5–15 (twelve times), 21:1–18 (twenty-five times), and 27:1–28:16 (thirty-four times), makes it almost certain. It is of course conceivable that some later writer inserted into his own record these passages from a 'travel diary' kept by one of Paul's companions. But why did not such a later author, and one so gifted, change the 'we' to 'they'? And would not some difference in vocabulary and style betray that one writer is quoting another's words?

We might prove that some companion of Paul wrote both these books if we could show in detail that everything Paul ever taught, wrote, or did, could be fitted exactly into the *Acts* story. This is not possible. Some details, like the several visits to Jerusalem which Paul mentions in *Galatians*, puzzle us, mainly because we do not know enough.

> *Acts* is by no means a complete 'history' of the apostolic church. Hundreds of miles of travel, and visits to important centres, are covered in two or three verses (18:18, 22–23, 20:1–3, 21:1–6). We hear nothing of the work of ten of the original apostles, or of the later story of the churches at Jerusalem, Antioch, Caesarea, or of the expansion of the church in Egypt, Ethiopia, or east of Palestine. *Acts* was written for its own purpose, and mentions only those people, places and events that are relevant to that purpose. A later writer would, we may be sure, make his account correspond at all points with Paul's known letters and movements. A companion sharing Paul's later life, but reviewing those years from a different viewpoint, would surely produce a story just as similar to, and just as different from, Paul's occasional references to his movements, as *Acts* is like, and unlike, the epistles.

Our incomplete information, in the same way, prevents our naming just one companion known to be with Paul at the times mentioned in the 'travel diary'. But those who have tried to sift through Paul's long list of colleagues for this purpose have usually concluded that Luke is the likeliest of all to have been with him at the relevant times.

Ancient Christian tradition is for once unanimous. It holds that Luke was the author of both books, and affirms this although Luke was not an apostle. One very old translation, and a later commentary, have at Acts 20:13 the words 'I, Luke, and those who were with me . . .'. And some early writers (Origen, Jerome for example) understood 2 Corinthians 8:18 — 'the brother whose praise is in the gospel throughout all the churches' — to refer to Luke and his written Gospel, although (so far as we know) the word 'gospel' was not used in that way in Paul's time. At best, these isolated opinions only illustrate the growing Christian tradition that Luke did write a Gospel.

The earliest clear statement on the subject is by Irenaeus (about AD 180), who quotes from almost every chapter of the Gospel, and who assumes without discussion that 'Luke, the follower of Paul, wrote it'. About the same time, a list of New Testament books drawn up by the church at Rome speaks of the Gospel of Luke the physician, the companion of Paul's journeying. Tertullian, from the church in north Africa, and Clement and Origen from the church in Egypt, support this opinion, and a prologue to an ancient Latin translation of the Gospel also gives Luke's name.

Luke was a physician (Colossians 4:14) and scholars once claimed to find perhaps four hundred 'medical-sounding' words in *Luke-Acts*, similar to the language of famous medical writers like Hippocrates (4th–5th century BC), and Galen (2nd century AD), so confirming that a 'doctor' was the author. But accurate checking of Luke's language against non-medical writers of the time has thrown doubt on this argument. It is now questioned whether there was a technical medical language in the first century, and Galen especially claimed to be using layman's terms. Consequently, cautious scholars today do not press this 'proof' that *Luke-Acts* was by Luke the physician.

For all that, some evidence of a medical man's outlook may be found in the Gospel — accurate observation for example. Luke describes miracles, diseases, and symptoms very precisely; he specifies a 'high' fever, 'full' of leprosy, and avoids calling haemorrhage 'a disease' as Mark does. And though Luke tells that story of the woman who had suffered long from haemorrhage, he omits Mark's statement that she 'had suffered much under many physicians, and had spent all that she had, and was no better but rather grew worse'.

All in all, we may be honestly satisfied that Luke did write our third Gospel, though he does not say so. There are certainly no other claimants.

But Who Was Luke?

Like all true evangelists, Luke says very little about himself. We have therefore to gather scattered clues to his character, and fill out the portrait with some mere probabilities. In speaking of him as a physician, we must not of course think of first-century doctors as scientists, but neither should we depreciate entirely their skill, responsibility, experience, and knowledge. Sirach (38:1–15) praises their skill and medicines as alike gifts of God. Their remedies included wine and oil for cleansing and soothing injuries (Luke 10:34), fig poultices, balm, myrrh, mint, cummin, and especially dietary recommendations like vinegar, wine, honey, almonds, figs. Circumcision and the isolation of infection, were common practices, and so was some elementary surgery. By his own writing, Luke is revealed as careful, competent by the standards of the first century, and very compassionate, certainly no fool, charlatan, or witch-doctor.

Colossians 4:14 with 11 shows Luke to be a Gentile. His use of the Greek Old Testament, his understanding of synagogue ways of thinking, and perhaps too his familiarity with Hebrew poetry (Luke 1–3), suggest that he was a proselyte to Judaism. But the phrase 'God-fearer' (or 'God-worshipper') occurs eight times in *Acts*. It was used to describe Gentiles attracted by the monotheism and morality of Judaism, but declining to become full proselytes because that would involve Jewish nationality, circumcision, and animal sacrifice. Luke's intense interest in this group, and in their reaction to the gospel, strongly suggests that he was once in their position. It is a little startling to realize that *the writer who contributed most to our New Testament was a Gentile, with a pagan, non-Judaist background, a representative of our own wider world beyond Jewry.*

Writing from prison, where Luke remained available to him (Colossians 4:14, 18, Philemon 24), Paul calls Luke 'beloved', and a 'fellow worker', tributes which breathe a sense of gratitude. We know that Paul sometimes needed medical care. To have won the affection of a man like Paul says much for Luke's personal qualities. If 2 Corinthians 8:18 refers at all to Luke himself (and that could explain the absence of Titus, there called Luke's brother, from the narrative of *Acts*), then another tribute must be added, 'praise in all the churches'.

Another obvious feature of Luke's character was strong independence of mind. Some have remarked the absence from Luke's writings of great Pauline ideas like justification by faith, law versus grace, the Christian's union with Christ in his death, the church as Christ's body. But Paul's many colleagues constituted an exceedingly varied company, by no means all imitators or sycophants. Barnabas, Peter, Mark, leaders at Corinth, and others, were able to differ from him without for long losing his friendship. Luke too could spend many months in Paul's company without becoming his mere echo. The Paul we know from his epistles is, by necessity and not by choice, the Paul of controversy and church problems; Luke shows another side of the apostle, the good and loyal Jew, taking Jewish vows, worshipping at the temple, paying dues and offering sacrifice (Acts 18:18, 20:16, 21:23–26, 23:6, 26:4, 5), while strongly resisting the imposition of Jewish law and customs upon Gentile Christians.

This independence of mind, the ability to admire without servility, might be sufficiently explained by Luke's different standpoint as a Gentile. But he was also, as all his writing shows, a man of cultured, orderly, meticulous mind (Luke 1:1–4 for example). He was a craftsman in language, his Greek the purest in the New Testament. He was much travelled, and of wide experience, far more interested in people than in ideas. Yet with all this strength and independence of judgement, Luke's loyalty to Paul is unquestioned; at the end (2 Timothy 4:11) Paul writes poignantly, 'Luke alone is with me'. No wonder Paul loved him!

For the rest, we have only attractive guesses, of varying plausibility. It is said that Luke was an artist, perhaps because of his vivid portrait-studies of Christians he met. From the enthusiasm of his writing, it has been inferred that 'Luke loved a good miracle', and also that he loved the sea. The infancy-songs in Luke 1–3 earned for Luke very early the reputation of a poet. It would be romantic to urge that the rare form of his name in Greek, 'Loukas', reveals a 'pet-name', formed from the 'upper class Latin name' Lucianus; and then argue that Luke was once a slave in some great house, trained in medicine (as some slaves were), and freed by a grateful master, whose name he borrowed in tribute! Equally romantic, unfortunately, is the suggestion that Loukas is the pet-form of Lucius, which might make Luke the Lucius of Cyrene of Acts 13:1, or even the 'kinsman' of Paul mentioned in Romans 16:21.

As to Luke's home, one early copyist of manuscripts asserts that Luke came from Antioch in Syria, and one Greek manuscript says at Acts 11:27, 'In those days prophets came down from Jerusalem to Antioch . . . and when we were assembled . . .' If this could be proved to be the original text, it would be the first 'we' passage from the 'travel diary'. Augustine and other early writers knew of this suggestion, and it is true that Luke manages to mention Antioch thirteen times. He describes the church there very vividly, and commends Barnabas enthusiastically for encouraging their work (Acts 11:22–24).

On the other hand, the first time Luke certainly uses 'we' is at Acts 16:10. It appears that there, at Troas, Luke met Paul and joined him, on the way to Philippi. It has been thought that Paul was too unwell to stay in humid Ephesus (Galatians 4:13–14 with Acts 16:9); if that be true, Luke's medical attention would be timely. After the Philippi adventure, Paul and Silas moved on into Macedonia, but Luke stayed behind (note 'they', not 'we' in Acts 16:40, 17:1). After visiting Thessalonica, Berea, Athens, and Corinth, Paul returned to Philippi, and Luke rejoined him (20:5 'we', and thereafter).

This long stay at Philippi may imply that the city was his home. Luke plainly dwells with special interest and detail on the Philippi story, and he takes obvious pride in Philippi as a very 'Roman' centre, a full 'colony' with special privileges, and a leading city in its district. Far less obvious, though attractive, is the theory that Paul, frustrated and perplexed by a series of closed areas, met the cultured doctor at Troas and talked with him about his home in Philippi, and the land of Greece beyond. Later, Paul dreamed of that conversation, and of 'a man of Macedonia . . . standing beseeching him and saying, "Come over to Macedonia and help us"'. If Luke was indeed the famous 'man of Macedonia', whose words opened Europe to the gospel, we wish he had not been too modest to tell us so. The story is left somewhat vague and unsatisfying (Acts 16:6–10).

That Luke remained beside Paul until his arrival at Rome, and later wrote *Luke-Acts*, completes Luke's story. A note on yet another ancient manuscript says that Luke died in Greece, unmarried, aged 84; which could be true, or mere gossip. What is certainly true is that, despite his modesty, Luke is revealed as a great Christian soul, faithful, loyal, useful, gifted, beloved; a Gentile, and therefore a detached observer of the Christian mission. Most surprising of all, this second-generation Christian, who never met Jesus, was not one of the original Twelve, nor a later apostle, recorded the life and ministry of Jesus against not a Jewish but a world background. *What is for many the most attractive and persuasive of all four Gospels was written by one who was not even there!*

It must be added at once that he had excellent qualifications for the work. Beside the years with Paul, Luke *may* have been in the church at Antioch, with Paul and Barnabas from the Jerusalem church, as early as AD 46. He was certainly present with Paul and Silas at Philippi around AD 50, travelled with Paul to Tyre and Ptolemais, where he met Palestinian Christians; then to Caesarea, where he met Philip the evangelist, one of the seven appointed in Jerusalem (Acts 6); there, too, very possibly, he met Mary the mother of Jesus, learning from her the infancy stories which only he records. He went on to Jerusalem, where he met James, the Lord's brother, and other elders. Luke spent AD 57–59 (approximately) in and around Jerusalem, making constant enquiries (as he tells us, Luke 1:1–4), seeking out eye-witnesses of Christ's ministry, and doubtless still making notes. He had also met with Mark, another Gospel-writer, when *Colossians* was written (Colossians 4:10, 14).

These were excellent opportunities for gathering and testing information, and Luke's early attachment to synagogue Judaism, his personal contacts, his qualities of mind, were splendid equipment for the task. Yet the most important qualification, and the most remarkable, was different again. It lay in his quite exceptional spiritual experience. His is the only Gospel to originate with one who first met Jesus *through the church*.

CHAPTER 2

Luke's Amazing Experience

Although Luke's prime qualification for writing of Jesus and the church was his personal experience of the truth of the gospel, we unfortunately do not know how, when, or where he became a Christian. But we do know that either at Antioch, or at Troas and soon afterwards at Philippi, Luke saw the living church at work.

Despite all our questions as to who actually put pen to papyrus, it is fairly certain that the apostle Matthew stands somewhere behind the Gospel of Matthew, the apostle Peter behind the Gospel of Mark, and the apostle John behind the Gospel that bears his name. Each saw at least some of the events to which he bore witness. Each moved forward from meeting Jesus in the flesh to seeing the church emerge and grow. But Luke, in the next generation of converts, and far from Palestine, first met the church, and by the church was introduced to Jesus. For him, as for every Christian since, the historical order of encounter was reversed. In this respect, Luke stands nearer to ourselves than could any of those who walked with Jesus in Galilee.

Luke's Conversion

All this makes us wish we did know exactly how Luke came to Christian faith. But if the circumstantial details are lost, we can perceive what in general Christian conversion meant to Luke, if we reflect cautiously upon what he writes of others' experience. For most of us find most interesting and credible those stories of Christian experience which resemble our own. Luke does not recount many conversions, and most of those only very briefly. Levi's story, and Lydia's, and that of Sergius Paulus, occupy only a verse or two. Some, like the conversion of Damaris, are merely mentioned.

The calling of Peter, James, and John is recounted in seven verses altogether; that of Zaccheus takes up ten verses, for a reason not difficult to explain. The dramatic conversion of the Philippian jailer also gets more extended description, though only five verses deal with the jailer's own reactions. Surprisingly, we learn no more of the conversion-experience of Barnabas (whom Luke admired so highly), of Stephen (whose speech and death take up much room in *Acts*), or of James the Lord's brother (so prominent in the apostolic church), than of that of Luke himself.

But three extended stories are recorded. Paul's conversion is described three times, occupying forty-three verses in all. Apart from Luke's close relation to the apostle, so vital a turning-point in the story of the early church demanded such analysis and emphasis. The story of the Ethiopian eunuch takes up fourteen verses. Most dramatic in itself, this story was also a clear instance of the operation of the Holy Spirit, who brought together Philip the evangelist and the Ethiopian in the wilderness, and then separated them again. Even more, the story was of special interest to a Gentile God-fearer like Luke. For the Ethiopian was a foreigner, yet returning from Jerusalem, reading the Old Testament, puzzled at some things in Judaism, wonderfully prepared for more illumination, and welcoming it with joy. We have every reason to think Luke felt close sympathy with an experience so like his own.

But the conversion of Cornelius is told in detail *twice*, and occupies Luke for *sixty-six* verses. Again the story was of immense importance, as illustrating the changing attitude of the apostolic church towards Gentile converts. But it was also, in several respects, essentially Luke's own story. For Cornelius, like Luke, was a Gentile, and devout, but still not a convert to Judaism — otherwise the whole argument about Peter's offering Christ to one 'unclean' would never have arisen (Acts 11). Cornelius was, too, a cultured man, a Roman officer in charge of a cohort of (nominally) a hundred men, with serious responsibilities different from, but at least as great as, Luke's own.

Luke dwells upon the story with care and evident enjoyment — the vision that prepared Peter, away in Joppa, to overcome his reluctance and learn to call nothing 'unclean' which God had 'cleansed'; Cornelius' own vision of the angel who brought such manifold assurance to his own heart, that his prayers had been heard and remembered by God; and that his generous almsgiving had been noted, too, in God's presence. He tells how God, knowing his continuing spiritual need, instructed him where to send for help. How the messengers arrived at Peter's door at the precise moment that the Spirit prepared Peter's mind. There follow the presentation of the Christian story, the explanation of the gospel, and the sudden exaltation of Cornelius and his fellow hearers in the power and joy of the Holy Spirit.

Then it is told all over again, defensively, but with a detail strictly unnecessary, except to one whose heart was warmed by it. As Luke's heart undoubtedly was.

To assume that Cornelius' experience deeply affected Luke because it closely resembled his own is no daring speculation. All we know of Luke tends to confirm that by some such steps he came into Christian commitment. No important truth may be deducible, but we can surely assume that Luke's meeting with Paul, just when he was ready for illumination, seemed to him as divinely-planned as Cornelius (and the

Ethiopian) had experienced. Some such assurance that his previous spiritual pilgrimage from paganism via the synagogue was accepted with God, came to Luke as to Cornelius. Some illumination broke upon his mind, as upon the mind of Cornelius, at the hearing of the gospel, and certainly some such confirmation in the joy and power of the Spirit. Though Luke will not talk about himself, his telling of Cornelius' testimony bears the clear stamp of his own.

The Church Luke Encountered

But if the details of Luke's conversion are unknown, the means by which it came about are written large throughout the book of *Acts*. At the most crucial period of his life, this cultured, observant, careful man, skilled in research, in writing, and in presentation of argument, with the temperament and ability to analyse clearly, and already devout, attracted to the best in Judaism, encountered the Christian church.

It happened possibly at Antioch, where amid a lively group of Christians, mainly Gentiles, inspired prophets uttered God's word, and the assembled company obediently did what the Holy Spirit directed. Or possibly at Troas, where Luke met Silas and Paul awaiting the leading of the same Spirit, and soon afterwards at Philippi, where the power of the Spirit convinced a pious, much-travelled business woman, transformed a possessed girl, shook the city to its foundations, converted overnight a responsible Roman civil servant, and reduced the proud magistrates to abject apology — the flogged and fettered apostles singing at midnight, meanwhile.

When Paul returned from the mission to Greece, Luke heard of the astonishing impact of the gospel in communities so different. 'What an entering in we had . . .' as Paul recalls, at Thessalonica, people 'turning from idols to serve the living and true God'. What success among the earnest, studious listeners at Berea. What a frigid reception, and limited results, but yet respectful hearing, at conceited Athens, intellectual capital of the world. And at Corinth, the cesspool of the empire, a cosmopolitan seaport filled with gambling dens, pagan shrines, prosperous vineyards from which wine flowed freely, the great temple of Aphrodite with its hundred brothels — here Christianity had confronted paganism at its coarsest and most degraded. Yet here, too, a church sprang into being, a dynamic congregation of men and women saved from vicious evils, and manifesting in abundance the marvellous 'gifts' of the Spirit in effervescent worship and infectious enthusiasm. We know that Luke learned all this, for he recorded it.

Later still, Luke heard, probably from the Ephesian elders themselves, of the mighty mission to Ephesus, the 'extraordinary miracles', the bonfire of magic spells and hoarded occult secrets, until the idol-makers staged a public protest at their loss of trade. And all this happened under the very shadow of the massive temple of Diana.

Then Luke travelled with Paul to the mother-church at the centre of the whole Christian movement, meeting on the way the four prophetesses, daughters of Philip, and Agabus, the impressive prophet from Jerusalem. The deep impression made by all this on Luke's devout and observing mind still glows in his vivid descriptions, and his pen-pictures of people. It is not difficult to analyse, from Luke's own writing, the separate ingredients of that total impression.

1. Whether at Antioch or at Troas, Luke realized he had fallen among people who lived under immediate divine direction. Resort to inspired 'oracles' was familiar enough; Romans venerated many kinds of sacred omens, divinations, prophecies, auguries, and prophetic dreams. But nothing in Luke's experience of paganism was so confident, or so creatively fruitful, as the obedience of Paul and others to the hinderings and promptings of an indwelling divine Spirit — 'Do not enter Bithynia . . .', 'Pass by Asia . . .', 'Go talk to Cornelius . . .' Nor had he met anything resembling the far-reaching initiatives of a whole group acting together, as at Antioch, at the bidding of the same Spirit — 'Separate me Barnabas and Saul . . .' Such experiences offered a wisdom for living far beyond man's own; such daily divine guidance made life under God's rule a practical and exhilarating possibility.

2. Later investigation only confirmed that divine superintendence was the normal expectation of these Christians. Whether evangelizing in the wilderness, as Philip did; breaking through old tabus about fellowship with Gentiles, as Peter did; consulting together over issues of church policy (Acts 15: 'it has seemed good to the Holy Spirit and to us . . .'); organizing mutual support (Acts 11:27–30); planning journeys (Acts 21:10–12); exercising oversight (Acts 20:28); or facing persecution (Acts 27:23–24), these resourceful people constantly depended upon the leading of an immanent 'Holy Spirit'.

Moreover, the effect of this superintendence by the Spirit was no fatalistic inertia, but a thrusting drive, always outwards and onwards. The first promise in *Acts* is 'You shall receive power when the Holy Spirit has come upon you, and you shall be my witnesses, in Jerusalem, and in all Judea, and Samaria, and to the end of the earth'. That is the programme of *Acts*, as it was the experience of Luke, at least as far as Rome. At each point of decision, at each setback or hesitation, the Spirit gave new impulse, direction, or confirmation (Acts 9:31, 10:9–23, 10:44, 11:15–18, 19:21, 20:22).

3. Essential to the practice of life under divine rule, Luke observed, was the cultivation of prayer. Guidance might come through scripture, by lot, in

trance, vision, or dream, but especially important was the Spirit's prompting and illumination within the prayerful heart, and the counsel of prophets within the group. By both means the divine will was regularly made known. Luke has very much to say, in both books, about prayer; and he was evidently much impressed by the phenomenon of prophecy, both Jewish and Christian, referring to it over fifty times.

4. Again, it is evident that Luke was 'surprised by joy' in the individuals and the assemblies of the church, in a somewhat forbidding world. Joy, courage, and great resilience mark the infant church as Luke described it. From the first Christian group, at home and in the Jerusalem temple, 'with glad and generous hearts, praising God'; the joy of one healed, 'walking and leaping and praising God'; and the 'great grace' upon them all, to the Christian response to official threats ('they left the presence of the council, rejoicing that they were counted worthy to suffer dishonour for the name'), and their reaction to actual persecution ('they shook off the dust from their feet against them, and . . . were filled with joy and with the Holy Spirit'), Luke felt a deep gladness of soul, a sustained exhilaration of spirit, ever welling up within his new colleagues. While convert after convert 'went on his way rejoicing'.

So constant and characteristic was this glad elevation of mood, that when Paul met certain 'disciples' at Ephesus who lacked it, he immediately enquired about the real meaning of their conversion and baptism. After instruction, he baptised them again, in the name of Jesus, setting right their deficiency.

5. As Luke learned more of the inner life of this new type of society, he was forcefully struck by the unique sense of 'koinōnia' or 'fellowship', 'partnership', cultivated among the varied members. The church had achieved the spontaneous creation of community. The first Christians were indeed an assorted collection, fishermen, civil servants concerned with taxation, a number of priests (Acts 6:7), Hellenists, Jews and proselytes, women of working and of courtly classes, from villages, cities, seashore and hills, rich and poor, slaves and free citizens. Yet they were welded into 'one heart and soul', with 'one accord' (Acts 4:31–32), to the extent of voluntarily sharing their goods, even selling family inheritance and distributing to those who through long poverty, or through loss of family support caused by conversion, stood in need.

'All who believed were together, and had all things in common', hospitality and generosity being the outward marks of intense unity of mind and feeling, cohesiveness, mutual loyalty and singleness of purpose. There were problems, of course, as when Hellenist Christians felt that Hebrew Christians were favoured in the distribution of help (Acts 6:1–6), or when avaricious greed sought to profit from the wave of generosity by holding back gifts while accepting support (Acts 5:1–11). But the promptness and effectiveness with which such problems were resolved illustrate how deep was that unity which the Spirit created and preserved. There were good reasons why Luke should draw his readers' special attention to this sign of the presence of the Spirit, a sign all the more significant in that church 'organization' was at this time minimal.

6. Looked at from without, however, this community's outstanding public feature was forceful, uninhibited speech, fearless, convincing, and authoritative (Acts 4:13, 33, 6:10). In a society familiar with interminable philosophical discussions, these men and women spoke as those who *knew*, from within, the truth of God. The earliest sign of the Spirit within the church (as Luke learned later) was the gift of prophecy, the impulse to speak forth divine truth with boldness, and the ability to communicate, and to convince, even across language barriers, as on the day of Pentecost. After long silence, the ancient prophetic inspiration had appeared again in the Baptist; now it was universalized, as old and young, servants and handmaids, sons and daughters, came to share in it by the gift of the Spirit. Less remarkable to us, perhaps, this phenomenon so perplexed the religious authorities in Jerusalem as to occasion special enquiry (Acts 4:13).

7. Attesting this bold witness there occurred manifestations of a more-than-human dynamism (Acts 1:8, 2:22, 4:7, 33, 8:10), which the apostles unhesitatingly disowned as due to any power or holiness of their own. Similar 'miracles' of healing, exorcism, and ecstatic speech, were claimed for many heathen shrines and sects, but Luke was evidently greatly impressed by the simplicity, variety, and plenitude of Christian acts of power, including resurrection (Acts 3:4–8, 9:36–42). He confesses to finding some of them (or their method) 'extraordinary' (Acts 19:11, 5:15 'even'); but that an immense reservoir of power was available and active within the Christian community was undeniable. Unexpected gifts of eloquence, shaken buildings, rushing winds, angel visitants, opened prisons, earthquakes, even sudden deaths (as of Ananias, Herod), made the church appear to live in the midst of miracle.

The first formal investigation into the new movement had demanded 'by what power or name' the disciples were ministering. The first recorded heresy attempted to purchase this apostolic energy. One startling comment, 'great fear came upon the whole church and upon all who heard these things . . . none of the rest *dared* join them' (Acts 5:11–13, 2:43) is fully justified by the stories of Ananias and Sapphira, and of Elymas. The divine energies at work were not to be trifled with. Moreover, as Luke's emphasis upon prayer, and upon the apostles' disclaimers, clearly shows, this power was invasive rather than inherent. Christians did not manipulate, but obeyed, the spiritual dynamic within them.

8. But Luke attached even greater importance to the enhancement of individual personality which he observed in the Christians he came to know. He parades a whole gallery of typical 'people of the Spirit': emotional, ebullient, vacillating yet tenacious Peter; John, overshadowed and quiet; the gifted and eloquent Hellenist, Stephen; practical and charitable Dorcas; generous, unselfish, essentially good Barnabas; wise and prayerful James; Silas, another gifted writer like himself, content to labour in others' shadows; devout and eager Lydia; the learned, academic yet passionate Paul; the talented Priscilla, apt to teach — and the rest, each exhibiting besides highly charged moral enthusiasm, the kindling of quite exceptional human abilities.

Luke found many ordinary people, of differing race, class, and background, to be exalted in spirit, redeemed in character, positive, confident, and creative, courageous and resilient, generous and loyal in fellowship, compassionate and welcoming towards outsiders. And, above and beyond all, joyous. At least twelve times Luke speaks of people 'full of holy spirit', as elsewhere he speaks of those 'full of' anger, fear, 'spirit and wisdom', 'faith and holy spirit'. From such a master of Greek, this turn of phrase seems deliberately to emphasize the 'fullness of holy spirit' (or enthusiasm) which is sure evidence of the Holy Spirit at work in the Christian personality. For Luke, such transformation of individuals constituted the greatest miracle of all, the answer to a decaying society's deepest problems.

Into this bubbling, seething cauldron of a church, this joyous, powerful, generous, exuberant, infectious, talkative eruption of religious thought, energy and fervour, walked Luke, the man of taste, education, training, and caution, like an honours student of history and psychology stumbling into a 'charismatic' convention. His first reaction must have been, 'What, in God's name, is going on?' His second reaction was, to be attracted, convinced, converted, wholly committed to this new lifestyle and movement. His third reaction was the desire to describe, explain, and commend this experience to others.

Luke himself had no doubt of the immediate explanation of these remarkable people he has met, of this fast-growing, morally creative and redemptive community he has encountered. These are men and women 'possessed', indwelt, and endued, by the living God, immanent in each as the Holy Spirit — or, as Luke says, very significantly, 'the Spirit of Jesus' (Acts 16:7). The ultimate explanation, however, was something to be sought further, in the movement's initial impetus and historical development.

This was the purpose of his Gospel, and of *Acts*, two books without which we should all be much the poorer. Yet Luke did not write for us, but for a particular group of his contemporaries, and they are steadily before his mind in every sentence he composes. Who are they?

CHAPTER 3

Luke's Audience

Unexpectedly, Luke addressed his commendation of Christianity to one 'Theophilus', and it seems strange that we know nothing about this man but what lies in the opening lines of Luke's Gospel, and of *Acts*.

> 'Inasmuch as many have undertaken to compile a narrative of the things which have been accomplished among us, just as they were delivered to us by those who from the beginning were eyewitnesses and ministers of the word, it seemed good to me also, having followed all things closely (margin: accurately) for some time past, to write an orderly account for you, most excellent Theophilus, that you might know the truth concerning the things of which you have been informed.'
>
> 'In the first book, O Theophilus, I have dealt with all that Jesus began to do and teach . . .'

By careful analysis of these phrases, by examination of the books' general contents, and from some knowledge of background circumstances, we have to try to fill out the portrait of Theophilus, and discover why Luke should design his work for him especially.

The New English Bible boldly makes the Gospel open with a formal literary 'dedication':

'THE AUTHOR TO THEOPHILUS: Many writers have undertaken . . .' This hardly represents the Gospel's first words in Greek; and though such dedication of literary work to prominent individuals, who might help to defray expenses and make the book known, was familiar in the ancient world, such an interpretation leaves all our questions unanswered.

Why to Theophilus?

'Theophilus' means either 'Lover of God' or 'Loved by God', and it could be understood as a pseudonym for 'the average Christian', or 'the typical convert'. But 'most excellent', and 'O Theophilus' sound very artificial if this is so. It is much more probable that he was a real person, and (from the form of his name) a fellow Gentile. This may be important, in understanding the place of Gentiles in both books.

Was Theophilus a Christian? Luke does not call him 'brother' (as Ananias called Saul, *during* his conversion, Acts 9:17). The two books together would seem a lot of 'first instruction' for a new convert. It is true that in Luke 1:4 the word 'informed' is the Greek term which later gave us 'catechumen', or 'enquirer under instruction'. This may be coincidence, or the later use may have arisen from this verse. But in truth, Luke wishes Theophilus to become *better* informed than he yet is — his instruction so far has been at fault.

Luke desires to give Theophilus an orderly and accurate account of Christianity, so that he may know the truth about the events of which so far he has had only inadequate information. The phrasing, though very polite, seems to imply that Theophilus has been sadly misinformed about the faith, and Luke wishes to put that right.

Especially intriguing is that epithet 'excellent', which Luke accords to Theophilus. It could mean simply 'best of men', expressing friendship, gratitude, admiration. But Luke uses the word three times in *Acts*, and we might expect consistency in such a writer. In 23:26, in a formal and official letter, it means '(to) His Excellency (the Governor Felix . . .)'; in 24:2, in personal address, it occurs as 'most Excellent Felix'; and in 26:25 as 'most Excellent Festus' (compare 'your Gracious Majesty . . .'). In all three places, the New English Bible translates 'Your Excellency', as also in Luke 1:3. We learn that the title distinguishes a Roman official of equestrian or higher rank, one holding government office. This would imply that Luke is addressing some aristocratic Roman of the class which he probably once served, and whom he desires shall know the truth about the Christian faith.

That by the time Luke wrote, Christianity had begun to gain the attention of the upper classes of the empire is well known. Only a little later, Christian epitaphs in Rome's catacombs provide sufficient evidence. Caesar's family, as well as his 'household', included converts. But the attitude of the educated and leading Romans was still on the whole sceptical, and, since Nero, hostile. After the fire of Rome, many other catastrophes were blamed upon Christians, and the growing insistence of the State upon worship of 'the spirit of Rome' bore hardly upon the Christian conscience. Increasingly slanderous reports about Christian 'superstitions' and practices created an antagonistic climate for Christian witness.

> In *Quo Vadis*, Henryk Sienkiewicz' fine novel about early Christianity, an aristocratic Roman registered dismay at discovering that the girl he sought was a Christian — 'Now just think, you are not a fool. Do you want us to believe that Pomponia and Lygia both belong to the sect of these enemies of mankind, these poisoners of fountains and wells, these worshippers of an ass's head, who sacrifice their children, and practise the most shameful debaucheries? Think man . . .'

That accurately reflects the attitude of upper class Roman society towards Christianity from the first century over the third. It rested mainly upon Christians' refusal to attend the temples, giving rise to the charge of atheism; upon the early secret 'love feasts' (assumed to be 'love-ins'); and upon the 'eating of flesh and drinking of blood in memory of Christ'.

It is not probable that Theophilus already believed such slanders, since Luke evidently thought he would read with some sympathy the books he was offering. But educated leaders of the Roman world heard and wondered about such reports, and were sometimes grossly misinformed about the faith upon which some of them had to sit in judgement. That is why we must notice with great care the defensive character of Luke's writings. Their content is not merely instruction, but firm Christian apologetic.

In *Acts* this is especially clear. So long as Christianity was regarded as a Jewish sect (24:5,14, 26:5, 28:22), it enjoyed the protection given to Judaism under Roman law. Throughout Paul's missions, Jewish attacks on Christianity were bitter, partly because of the new faith's success among the God-fearers on the fringe of the synagogues. Jews stigmatized Christianity as renegade, and everywhere sought to embroil Christians with the authorities. Theophilus well represents the attracted but perplexed attitude of such magistrates and governors in this situation.

Luke plays down the sharper differences between Judaism and Christianity, emphasizing that it was Jewish *mobs* that caused the trouble. He shows Christianity the natural heir to all that was best in Judaism, without its nationalism, exclusiveness, or bigotry. Peter, Stephen and Paul expound at length the true relation of the new faith to the old, which such as Theophilus will want to hear. He shows how, through events, God led from Judaist origins to a universalist faith; how groundless was the Jewish charge of sedition. He illustrates Paul's faithfulness to the Jewish scriptures, feasts and nation, only abandoning the synagogues when thrown out. The Jewish scholar Gamaliel, and Agrippa, the specialist adviser on Jewish affairs, were tolerant of Christianity, and the Jews at Rome have no accusation to make, and receive Paul peaceably. In fact, so Luke is arguing, Christianity deserves still to share in Judaism's legal status.

As to the church's relation to Rome, a whole list of Roman judicial authorities have already declared Paul innocent of any offence against the State — the deputy on Cyprus; the jailer and the magistrates at Philippi; the politarchs at Thessalonica; Gallio — brother to the great Seneca — a consul at Corinth; the asiarchs at Ephesus, led by the town-clerk; Claudius Lysius, the Roman Commander at Jerusalem; Felix, the Governor at Caesarea; Festus, who replaced Felix; and Herod Agrippa, official policy consultant. This was a series of precedent acquittals to satisfy any Roman tribunal trying Christians in any part of the world. And all this Luke lays before His Excellency Theophilus, as the case for Christianity.

So much is clear in *Acts*, but the Gospel reveals the same defensive stance. The opening paragraph concedes that some current accounts of the origin of Christianity have been unsatisfactory, and urges the 'eye-witness' basis of Christian testimony, Luke's own prolonged investigation and effort to produce an accurate and orderly account, so laying 'the truth' before Theophilus. Thus he prepares his evidence.

At once, with great skill, Luke launches into the stories of the birth of John and Jesus, directly in line with the prophetic tradition and the finest domestic piety of Judaism, fulfilling the past. At the end, when Jewish malice had (Luke shows) done its worst, an educated and responsible Jew, a member of the Jewish Council, a good and righteous man, who had not consented to the deed of the leaders or the mob, treated Jesus' body with utmost respect.

Jesus' own relations with Romans in Palestine were uniformly good. He had commended a Roman centurion's faith and healed his slave. He won from another centurion, by the courage with which he faced death, the high commendation, 'Certainly this man was innocent!' Jesus counselled support for the State, and the payment of Caesar's tax demands. He acted swiftly in Gethsemane to quell any impulsive attempt at armed resistance to law. And he was *four times* declared innocent of crime, both privately and publicly, by the Roman judges on the spot — by Pilate the Governor, by Herod the titular 'king' in Galilee, and by Pilate again, and yet again (23:4, 6–15, 14, 22).

Luke makes very clear (23:5, 18, 21, 23) that only the clamour of the Jewish crowd made it expedient for Pilate, although he desired to release Jesus, to 'deliver Jesus up to their will'. 'Their voices prevailed': every Roman magistrate would at least understand Pilate's dilemma, if not approving of his decision. Luke leaves no possible doubt that Jesus was innocent, yet makes no accusation against Pilate, or against Roman justice. Rome, Luke insists, has nothing to fear from Jesus, nor from the church.

Since this careful and very full defence of Christianity is addressed to 'Your Excellency Theophilus', it is at least possible that Theophilus was himself a judge, or magistrate, officially involved in assessing the legality of Christianity as a new religion, a new moral force, or a new political group. Be that as it may, it is well-nigh certain that Theophilus represented in his own person that whole Roman governing class, aristocratic, cultured, responsible, upon whom, humanly speaking, the future of Christianity and the safety of Christians would depend. Luke's books were certainly not intended for private possession only. Theophilus is but first, and typical, of the kind of influential people whom Luke wants to reach. He is one individual, known to Luke, through whom he addresses a whole stratum of society.

This was, in some respects, a new area of evangelism for the church, different from Jewish congregations in the synagogues, from the very mixed community of Corinth, from the intellectuals of Athens, and from the slave population which the gospel strongly attracted. The new hearers needed a new approach, careful, soundly based and argued, educated, even literary, and this is just what Luke attempted. He would describe the Christian experience, commend the Christian gospel, and defend the Christian record, in the best way he could, and dispel the tendentious 'misinformation' which some of Theophilus' friends might be all too ready to believe.

This conclusion concerning the kind of audience Luke has in mind will tend so to colour our understanding of the Gospel and its purpose that we should enquire whether any other features of Luke's work, beside the probabilities about Theophilus, and the strongly defensive tone of both books, lend confirmation to the argument. The main evidence will lie, of course, in the detailed study of what Luke has to say, but certain secondary features of his work may be noticed meanwhile.

A Well Fashioned Missile
1. Glancing yet again at that opening sentence of the Gospel, we recall the expert opinion that it is expressed in 'the purest classical Greek in the whole of early Christian literature'. Most of the New Testament is written in the Greek of the market place and the street, often mixed with Aramaic words and ways of speech. But Luke's language is cultivated, stylistic Greek. For a few examples: Mark can write of the paralytic's 'pallet' (or hay-sack), and of Christ's 'carcase'; Luke corrects these to 'couch', 'body'. Mark speaks of Jairus' 'lass', Luke of a 'maiden'; Mark mentions a 'kenturion' (which is Latinized-Greek slang); Luke makes it 'Commander of a hundred'.

Luke uses a far wider vocabulary than other New Testament writers, and handles it more flexibly, finding the right word for the right place. Jews sound like Jews, in his pages, Romans like Romans; official letters and speeches sound official, and the songs in Luke 1–3 are in excellent Hebrew poetic style, though their language is now Greek. All that this means is, that for the special task of presenting the gospel to educated, cultured minds, which could be offended by uncouth language, God chose a scholarly Gentile physician, with the knowledge and training that fitted him for the work.

2. Luke's writing is also memorably beautiful. The Magnificat and Nunc Dimittis have entered Christian worship all over the world; a score of passages — the shepherds' story, Jesus' boyhood, Jesus at Nazareth, 'consider the lilies . . .', the prodigal, the Samaritan, the Pharisee and the publican, the storm at sea, the walk to Emmaus — live in every Christian's memory. Luke's penmanship is varied, vital and vibrant, the style 'sweetly reasonable', melodious, always lucid. Luke's ability to describe scenes and people makes them live before us. It is obvious that Luke wrote for an audience with intelligence and taste to appreciate his narrative power, dramatic contrasts, and attractive manner.

3. Luke's orderliness, and striving for accuracy, reveal a degree of historical sense, always the mark of an educated mind. Jesus is set against a world background (Luke 3:1–3). In *Acts*, Luke is scrupulously correct in the titles he gives to local officials; in both books events are usually so linked as to show development, step by step, in the unfolding story. Little in social conditions or personal history is ultimately causeless, and leaders responsible for justice or for local government would appreciate Luke's understanding.

4. A certain 'biographical' interest also marks the educated mind, and did so in the ancient world. Not, indeed, in the modern sense of psychological analysis and 'explanation' of people, but as an intense interest in individuals, their motivation, and the interplay of people with events, their conversation, and reactions to experience. Those who at any level have to rule others need to understand them, and Luke's interest, not only in 'people of the Spirit' but in Roman officials, Zechariah an aged priest, John the Baptist, the demoniac of Gadara, Joseph of Arimathea, Gamaliel, Martha and her sister, Simon Magus, contrasted figures like the prodigal and his elder brother, the Pharisee and the tax collector, Jesus and the penitent thief — the list of Luke's 'characters' is almost endless — would be shared by his readers. And especially, of course, his passionate interest in the person of Jesus, so exquisitely drawn, and so perennially attractive as Luke presents him.

It is significant that Luke draws special attention to manliness, courage, and strong-mindedness, which Romans were taught to value above all qualities. In *Acts*, both Stephen and Paul exhibit this quiet heroism in suffering, shipwreck, and death. In the Gospel, Christ's resolute advance towards Jerusalem with its dangers; his repeated, open-eyed warnings of coming tragedy; his rejection of impulsive offers of allegiance, spelling out the high cost of discipleship, are all clues to an attitude of mind which Luke's readers would note and appreciate.

Especially, perhaps, would they relish Jesus' repeated call to prepare for self-discipline and self-denial. Stoics were often blamed for hiding or repressing family affection; Jesus' demand to 'hate' father or mother for the sake of the kingdom would occasion no such difficulty to them as it does to modern Christians. So with Jesus' challenge to take up the cross 'daily' (only Luke has that significant word), and to count well beforehand the cost of building your tower of idealism, of waging your conflict with opposition, before you embark upon enterprises you may not be able to complete. For the prevailing, home-spun philosophy of the Roman legions was mainly the Stoic training to decide carefully, hold tenaciously, and conceal all fear, pain, and regret, as contemptible weakness.

5. It is surprising to learn how deeply superstitious the great Romans were, despite their reputation for rational practicality. Not omens and soothsayers alone, but witchcraft, spells, demon possession, the signs the gods gave, such as falling buildings, the flight of birds, earthquakes, comets, and much else, all capable of diverse interpretation, could affect decisions of statecraft, reverse battles, strike panic into rulers and people alike. 'The gods' were everywhere and everywhere unpredictable, powerful, sometimes implacable. In consequence, any sign or threat of the supernatural exercised enormous power over the Romans' imagination.

Luke is fully aware of this as he stresses constantly the supernatural powers released with Christianity, the voices, signs, healings, earthquake, eclipse, wind, and the constant activity of the living Spirit of God, in conversion or in judgement, that attended the progress of the church. It was not only that Luke himself was deeply impressed by the supernatural energy at work through the gospel, but that he knew that his readers would be highly susceptible to such influences. They would not miss the clear warning of Gamaliel, not to be found fighting against God, to be very careful what they did to Christians under direct divine protection.

Such secondary features of Luke's writings only tend to support his major emphases and interests in confirming that he has in his 'mind's eye' a section of society not hitherto reached directly by the growing church, a section whose sympathetic understanding and judgement might prove literally *vital* in the coming years. They could properly appreciate his qualities as a writer, and the case he had to present. His Gospel and its sequel are extremely well fashioned missiles for the target at which he aims. *Luke* is a cultured Gospel for a cultured class, produced by the mind of a historian, the pen of a poet, in the language of a scholar with the heart of a Christian, to commend Christianity to people like Theophilus.

CHAPTER 4

Luke's Explanation

To recapitulate briefly: The cautious and cultured Gentile, Luke, having undergone a transforming experience and met some remarkable people within the Christian movement, has set himself to describe, explain and commend Christianity to the 'upper levels' of Roman society, fitly represented by 'His Excellency, Theophilus'. Luke is aware that many of this circle have distorted views of the Christian movement, and also that, to a large extent, the future of the church may depend, officially and socially, upon their understanding and good will.

The Age of the Spirit
The immediate explanation of the church Luke had come to know and admire, of the people who intrigued him, and of the astonishing events he had witnessed, lay in the direct inspiration of individuals by the Holy Spirit of God. The ultimate explanation, according to the story these people told, lay in the appearance in history of Jesus of Nazareth. With him the whole Spirit-led movement originated, to him it testified, from him it derived its ongoing life. The Spirit that possessed these Christians, and energized and superintended this church, was — 'the Spirit of Jesus' (Acts 16:7). To explain the movement, therefore, Luke had to research and record the story of this Jesus. Luke had other purposes also in mind, but this was the order of his discovery and the process of his thought. He wrote his Gospel retrospectively, tracing back to Jesus the rise of that quality of life, and of group activity, which had so deeply impressed him.

This, then, is how the whole marvellous Spirit-filled movement started: the Holy Spirit came upon a young girl in Nazareth, in a little-known corner .of the Roman empire, the district of Galilee in the province of Syria. In due course, this Jewish peasant girl gave birth to one filled with the Spirit of God, who eventually imparted the Spirit to all who followed him. So was born the church.

It is illuminating to pick out the recurrent phrases by which Luke keeps this theme constantly before his readers:

The preparation of the forerunner, John — 'He will be great before the Lord

. . . he will be filled with the Holy Spirit even from his mother's womb.'

The conception of Jesus within Mary's womb — 'The Holy Spirit will come upon you, and the power of the Most High will overshadow you; therefore the child to be born will be called holy, the Son of God.'

The prophesying of John's father at John's birth — 'And his father Zechariah was filled with the Holy Spirit and prophesied . . .'

Elizabeth greets the unborn Jesus — 'Elizabeth . . . filled with the Holy Spirit . . . exclaimed . . . "Blessed you are among women, and blessed is the fruit of your womb!"'

The recognition of Jesus by people filled with the Spirit — 'Simeon . . . righteous and devout . . . and the Holy Spirit was upon him. And it had been revealed to him by the Holy Spirit that he should not see death before he had seen the Lord's Christ. And inspired by the Spirit he came into the temple . . . took him up in his arms and blessed God . . .' 'And there was a prophetess, Anna . . . and coming up at that very hour she gave thanks to God . . .'

The Baptist's promise — 'John answered . . . "I baptise you with water; but he who is mightier than I is coming . . . he will baptise you with the Holy Spirit and with fire."'

Jesus endued with the Spirit — 'When Jesus also had been baptised and was praying, the heaven was opened, and the Holy Spirit descended upon him in bodily form as a dove . . .'

Jesus led to temptation — 'And Jesus, full of the Holy Spirit, returned from the Jordan and was led by the Spirit for forty days in the wilderness, tempted by the devil.'

Jesus returns home — 'And Jesus returned in the power of the Spirit into Galilee . . . And he taught in their synagogues . . .'

Jesus begins his ministry — 'And he came to Nazareth . . . and he went into the synagogue . . . and he stood up to read . . . "The Spirit of the Lord is upon me . . ." And he began to say to them, "Today this scripture has been fulfilled in your hearing."'

Jesus exults — 'In that same hour he rejoiced in the Holy Spirit and said, "I thank thee, Father . . ."'

Jesus on prayer — 'If you, then, who are evil, know how to give good gifts . . . how much more will the heavenly Father give the Holy Spirit to those who ask him?'

Jesus on persecution — 'When they bring you before the synagogues . . . rulers . . . authorities . . . the Holy Spirit will teach you in that very hour what you ought to say.' .

Jesus' promise for the future — 'And behold, I send the promise of my Father upon you; but stay in the city, until you are clothed with power from on high . . . You shall receive power when the Holy Spirit has come upon you.'

The intention, and the emphasis, of these eighteen references to the Holy Spirit are unmistakable. Luke represents the coming and ministry of Jesus as the advent of one Spirit-laden, and the source of the Spirit for the church. In truth, he interprets Christ in the light of his later experience of the church as he knew it. This is so important that its implications deserve to be spelled out in some detail.

The Bearer of the Spirit

Luke begins the story of Jesus where apostolic preaching usually began, with John the Baptist, 'filled with the Holy Spirit' from his birth. Luke associates this enduement with the reawakening of prophecy in Israel, since in his experience in the church, prophecy was essentially a function of the Spirit. Luke then introduces, together in one sentence, Jesus, and the Spirit as the personal agent of the Most High in preparing for the birth of Jesus. When Mary visits her kinswoman, Elizabeth too is inspired to prophesy by the Holy Spirit who 'fills' her; at the birth of John, Zechariah, also filled with the Holy Spirit, breaks into prophecy. The age of the Spirit is dawning.

So, in turn, Jesus the child born of the Spirit is recognized and hailed by people of the Spirit. First Simeon, endued, promised this privilege of seeing the Christ, and prompted — all 'by the Spirit' — broke into poetic prophecy. Then Anna, 'a prophetess' and so another person of the Spirit, greeted Jesus in prophetic terms. The superintendence of the Spirit over all that was happening was as clear to Luke in these details as it was in the life of the later church. Yet, keeping close to historic fact, Luke does not suggest any endowment of the Spirit upon the growing boy.

That endowment occurred at Christ's baptismal commissioning. Here, Luke's references to the actual baptism, and to Jesus' praying, are grammatically subordinate to the main statement, namely that the heavens opened, the Holy Spirit descended, and a voice spoke. It is at first sight surprising that one born of the Spirit should need any further endowment of the Spirit in baptism, until we appreciate Luke's loyalty to historic truth. The baby and the boy were not 'infant prodigies'; and we do not know just when, or how clearly, awareness of his unique destiny dawned upon Jesus. What we do know is what Jesus himself must have told at some time, for Mark makes the baptismal experience private to the Master himself (Mark 1:10–11).

And that is, that baptism brought at any rate a final and complete assurance that Jesus was God's royal Son and servant (the 'voice' echoes Psalm 2:7, Isaiah 42:1). It brought also a fuller endowment of the Spirit than had been necessary or appropriate during childhood and youth. The four phrases, 'the Spirit . . . descended', 'full of', 'led by' (Mark says 'drove', almost implying control), and 'the power of the Spirit' (Luke 3:22, 4:1, 14) suggest respectively the moment of endowment, the greater measure, the directing guidance, and the manifest authority and force, which now became public. The first outward sign of the change was that Jesus never returned to the former life at Nazareth: the ministry had begun.

For Luke, of course, this whole baptismal incident had the greater importance because he had often seen such baptisms, followed by evidence of the Spirit's presence, in the churches he knew. He saw a correspondence between Christ's experience and that of his fellow Christians, and though he does not make a point of it, in effect he founds the church's practice of baptism upon the historic baptism of Jesus.

Jesus returned from Jordan 'full of the Holy Spirit' and was 'led by the Spirit for forty days in the wilderness', being tempted. Luke's choice of tense, and the whole expression, indicates that the Spirit continued to lead Jesus throughout the forty days; at the end, 'the devil departed', but not the Spirit. The curious conjunction of phrases in 4:1–2 'led by the Spirit . . . tempted by the devil' immediately sets the scene (whether Luke so intended or not) for the whole of Christ's ministry and the life of the church. In Christ's presence in history to redeem, a confrontation and a conflict are involved, a more-than-human struggle is going on. The Holy Spirit and the spirit of evil clash in the wilderness, and continue to do so throughout Luke's two-volume story. Thus Luke consistently represents Jesus as the bearer of the Spirit, with whom the new age of the Spirit, promised by Isaiah (11:1–2, 42:1, 44:3) and Joel (2:28–29), has opened.

In recounting the story of Christ's ministry, Luke is less free to express his own viewpoint, since the main outlines of events were already fixed. But in four features Luke does emphasize Christ's relation to the Spirit. Thus, pausing only to remark that Jesus returned from his temptation 'in the power of the Spirit', Luke chooses to open the story with the scene at Nazareth, although (as 4:23 reveals) Jesus had already been ministering at Capernaum. By so doing, Luke records, as the very first public words of Jesus, the significant announcement 'the Spirit of the Lord is upon me'. The ministry so announced was then characterized, in Isaiah's words, as acceptable to the poor, the captive, the blind, the oppressed, precisely the features of the church's ministry to the disadvantaged and the needy which had so impressed Luke. *Power channelled by compassion* was henceforth to be the hallmark of the Spirit's presence, alike through Jesus and in the church.

Secondly, Luke emphasizes the prophetic aspects of Christ's ministry. In answer to 'Is not this Joseph's son?' Jesus himself cited the precedents of Elijah and Elisha, so at once authorizing a prophetic interpretation of his mission. At Nain, the crowd glorified God, saying 'A great prophet has arisen among us'. Simon the Pharisee pondered whether this prevalent assessment of Jesus could possibly be true, and so did Herod. The disciples reported to Jesus that this was the popular estimate of him, and he himself declared that he must go to Jerusalem because no prophet could perish elsewhere. Two disciples walking to Emmaus express Luke's own summary of the story: 'Concerning Jesus of Nazareth, who was a prophet . . . mighty in deed and word.'

Prophecy being to Luke a foremost manifestation of the inspiring Spirit, to be 'mighty in word' was the Spirit's unmistakable accent. The boldness and power which Luke had felt in the apostolic testimony corresponded to the self-evident and unanswerable authority of Jesus himself, in his teaching, healings, exorcisms, and forgiveness, as one man, a centurion trained to authority, eloquently testified.

But, thirdly, Jesus was 'mighty in deed' too. The first recorded miracle of the ministry was, according to Luke, an exorcism. This again involved the explicit confrontation of 'unclean spirits' with the power of the Holy Spirit (4:34–36). Unclean, evil, harmful spirits are mentioned eleven times by Luke, and Jesus' encounters with them seven times. At one point Jesus was charged with being in league with the spirits, so obvious was their surrender to him. One of his own descriptions of his exorcisms likens them to the invasion of a strong man's house by one stronger than he, making spoil of his possessions (11:14–27, compare 10:17–21). Luke makes use of Christ's saying about devils that return to repossess the souls from which they have been banished, apparently to imply the positive superiority of Jesus' exorcisms over the merely negative exorcisms of current practitioners. It is fairly clear that Luke thinks of exorcism alone as insufficient, unless positive possession by the Holy Spirit of all good replaces the demons driven out.

In *Luke*, moreover, there is something majestic about Christ's domination of the spirit-world, in the simplicity of the miracle which followed the transfiguration, in the *many* 'troubled with unclean spirits' but now cured (6:18), in the quiet sanity of the man at Gerasa, in the deliverance from *sevenfold* possession of Mary of Magdala. The comment at 4:35, that 'the demon . . . came out . . . having done him no harm' applies to all Christ's exorcisms in *Luke*; the agonized writhing and groaning are always part of the symptoms, not of the cure. Such triumph over evil possession, in Jesus as in the church, would especially impress Luke the physician.

And, fourthly, exorcism was only one example of energies resident in Jesus which Luke found almost beyond description. When (like the apostles later) Jesus was investigated by an official deputation, they discovered only that 'the power of the Lord was with him to heal' (5:17–26). Luke shared the crowds' astonishment at the 'mighty powers' (or 'majesty') of God manifest in Jesus (9:43, 4:36, 5:9). The lasting impression of a single day spent in Christ's company was 'We have seen strange things today!' (5:26).

Certain details make this impression of measureless power extraordinarily vivid. 'All the crowd sought to touch him, for power came forth from him and healed them all' (6:19). A woman touched the fringe of his garment and was healed; Jesus touched a leper, and 'immediately his leprosy left him'. Jesus' vibrant personality infused divine energies into other lives, and so evident was this dynamism that on occasion 'fear seized them all' (7:16, compare Acts 2:43, 5:13). Herod thought Jesus was the Baptist risen from the dead — what must the personal force of Jesus have been to lend credibility to such an idea?

Yet this was the power which Luke discovered about him in the apostolic church. He makes the connection between Jesus and the later experience perfectly plain when he reports Peter's words uttered to Cornelius, 'God anointed Jesus of Nazareth with the Holy Spirit and with power; . . . he went about doing good and healing all that were oppressed by the devil, for God was with him.' It is no exaggeration to describe Luke's Gospel, as the elaboration of that summary. In Luke's own remarkable figure of speech, 'the finger of God' was stirring that generation (11:20; Matthew reports the saying as 'by the Spirit of God' 12:28). Jesus moved among men as the vehicle and bearer of the 'Spirit of might', as promised by Isaiah (11:2).

The Bestower of the Spirit

Yet this power of the Spirit was not intended for Jesus only, even during his lifetime. Luke notes certain clear foregleams of the church's future experience. As John had said, baptising 'with the Holy Spirit' was to be the distinguishing mark of the Christ who was coming. This is an enigmatic saying, but so Luke appears to have understood John's words, as a *promise* of the Spirit to others (see 3:16, Acts 1:5, 11:16, 19:3–6). The historical circumstances of John's announcement, before Christ's ministry had begun, before Christ's own teaching on the Spirit, show that they could hardly mean, when spoken, all that Christians later came to read into them. John's disciples in Acts 19 had 'never even heard that there is a Holy Spirit' — in the way in which a Christian apostle used the term. John's utterance had been a *warning* that the coming Messiah would purify the nation's outward life with axe, flail, shovel and flame, and its inner life by the 'spirit of judgement and by a spirit of burning' (compare Isaiah 4:4, Malachi 3:2–3, 4:1). By Luke's time, the phrasing carried to Christian hearts the promise of Pentecost (as Acts 1:5), and the Christian experience of baptism tended to confirm this interpretation of John's words. The Christ would baptise others with the Spirit that was upon himself.

But the expectation was not due entirely to hindsight. Already, as the disciples were sent out upon their earlier missions, Jesus bestowed upon them 'power and authority over all demons and to cure diseases', 'authority to tread upon serpents and scorpions, and over all the power of the enemy' (9:1, 10:19). Looking to the coming years, Jesus promised that in days of persecution and judicial examination, the Spirit would inspire the defence to be made 'in that very hour' (12:11–12, 21:14–15). The phrasing of this promise might well have provided the seed-thought which developed later into the full Christian doctrine of the Spirit as advocate, intercessor, 'paraclete'.

The solemn words 'Every one who speaks a word against the Son of man will be forgiven; but he who blasphemes against the Holy Spirit will not be forgiven', are made more difficult in Luke (12:10) by being separated from what appears to be their original context, the 'blasphemy' that Jesus worked by the help of Satan. That accusation revealed a moral blindness, an inability to distinguish good from evil, that sets a man beyond self-understanding, beyond repentance, and so beyond forgiveness (see Matthew 12:23–32). For Luke, the saying evidently constituted a warning against the dire responsibility of rejecting the Christian testimony in the crucial age of the Spirit. In the days of Christ's humiliation, unbelief might be excusable, or at least understandable (so Luke seems to interpret the words); after Pentecost, unbelief and blasphemous rejection would be indefensible, and must prove unpardonable.

The familiar saying 'If you know how to give good gifts . . . how much more will your Father . . . give good things to those who ask him?' ends, in Luke's version, '. . . give the Holy Spirit to those who ask him?' (11:13). The change must be deliberate, and it illumines again Luke's preoccupation in the Gospel with the coming age of the Spirit, and the close relation of that experience of the Spirit with the practice of prayer, which he had often observed in the apostolic church. To Luke, the greatest of all the 'good things' put within our reach by the redemptive work of Christ was the gift of the Spirit, the fountain of so much else.

Another 'foregleam' of the truth that the bearer of the Spirit will in future prove to be also the bestower of the Spirit, is yet clearer. In Luke 24:49 the whole gospel story is made to lead up to 'the promise of the Father', that the disciples should in their turn be endued with power from on high. They are to wait in Jerusalem until they are 'clothed with power', which Acts 1 reveals to be 'when the Holy Spirit has come' upon them.

So at six distinct points the Gospel anticipates the coming of the Spirit upon the church in authority and power. To account for the Spirit-filled church Luke has taken us back to the Spirit-born, Spirit-bearing, Spirit-bestowing Christ, explaining the church he knew so well by the Christ he never met. Mark sketched a vivid, factual, excited account of Jesus, with all the marks of an eye-witness. Matthew presents Jesus in Jewish terms, appealing to a later generation of the nation which rejected him not to repeat that mistake. John based upon Christ's story a theological and evangelistic tract — 'that you might believe that Jesus is the Christ, and believing have life through his name'. Luke has shown us the Christ behind the Christian experience, the origin of the changed lives, the confidence and joy, the power and the hope, of the living church.

Of course Luke has more to say about Jesus, and he will go on to show why the experience of the Spirit which Jesus initiated is so important to his readers and to society. But his assessment of Jesus, while not exhausted by the terms Spirit-bearer and Spirit-bestower, does begin there, with one far-reaching consequence which must not be overlooked. The Spirit of God had been known in Old Testament experience as the invisible power of God at work in Nature and in man, producing sometimes odd results like Saul's dancing naked on the hillside, and Samson's exploits with the jawbone of an ass. But the Spirit produced also the wonderful prophetic tradition of theological insight and ethical realism.

Paul, we know, personalized and moralized the earlier conception of the Spirit as 'the Spirit of Christ'. But it was Luke who (so far as records show) coined the phrase 'the Spirit of Jesus', worked out the correspondence between the person and mission of Jesus and the Christian experience of the Spirit, and so rooted the church's experience in the story of Jesus that never again can the church be satisfied with an idea of the Spirit as mere power, or 'spiritual influence'. 'The Spirit of Jesus' is no divine magician, no purveyor of signs and wonders and provider of thrills, nor is he to be manipulated by human 'faith'. We know the Spirit, now, from his manifestation in Jesus. And that means that the one infallible criterion of the Spirit's presence in the church, or in a Christian, is *Christlikeness* — nothing less.

Having pointed back to Jesus as the origin of the Christian movement, Luke is committed to telling his story, and to explaining his significance. To his skill in so doing we now turn.

CHAPTER 5

An Overview

To obtain a conspectus of Luke's Gospel it is necessary to attempt an outline, but also dangerous. Outlines of Bible books are usually subjective inventions, and the danger lies in assuming that such a scheme was in the mind of the writer, and then making every paragraph fit somehow into the predetermined programme. The very simplest outline of Luke avoids this:

A: Introduction (1–3)
B: Ministry in Galilee (4:1–9:50)
C: Ministry in Judea (9:51–24:53)

but even that has difficulties. For B includes several references to Judea, before Jesus even visits there (4:44, 5:17, 6:17, 7:17 although Nain was near Capernaum in Galilee). It is true that Luke sometimes uses 'Judea' the Roman way, as meaning 'Palestine' (1:5, 23:5 where 'Judea' includes Galilee!). That the main emphasis in B concerns Galilee, and that of C concerns movement towards the south and ministry there, is clear enough. Unfortunately such an 'outline' is not very illuminating.

At the opposite extreme is an attempt to show that the Gospel has three main divisions; under the first and second are six subdivisions, and under the third three; and then under *each* of these fifteen subdivisions there are exactly six sub-subdivisions. Why any writer, not to say one so skilled as Luke was, would ever want to arrange his work in this artificial way, passes comprehension. It is said that Jewish rabbis arranged lectures on this plan, but Luke was no rabbi, and not even a Jew. Only a highly computerized, skilfully programmed word-processor would ever tell a story in this fashion.

A Tentative Outline

It is far safer to observe what the Gospel contains, and let whatever 'arrangement of material' there may be emerge of itself, tidily or otherwise. If we isolate and number the separate 'items' (events, sayings, parables, genealogy) which Luke records, we find about 154. After the brief 'preface' or dedication, twelve paragraphs deal with the background and birth of John and Jesus respectively; these plainly had to come first. Equally obviously, the first public appearances of John and of Jesus occur next, with the genealogy of Jesus appended. At 4:1 Christ's ministry begins with a review of alternative methods, the issue of a 'manifesto' at Nazareth, and removal to Capernaum. So far Luke's order is fairly close to that of Matthew and Mark, except for the story of Christ's boyhood and the place allotted to the sermon at Nazareth. But the order could hardly be otherwise; it is how things happened.

Much the same must be said about the last forty-two paragraphs, and especially the last twenty-five or so. A prophecy of death, the journey through Jericho, entry to Jerusalem, cleansing the temple, challenge to the city, discourse on the future, the betrayal, the last supper, the agony, the denial by Peter, mockery, trial, death, and resurrection, could hardly be dealt with in any other order. Luke tells much which the other Gospels omit, and tells all in his own way, but the arrangement is fixed by the story itself.

But between this logical beginning and end is a long middle portion of Luke (5:1–18:38), containing more than half of what Luke has to say (some 86 sections out of his 154), in which it is difficult to discover any arrangement at all. Some items — the call of Peter, James and John; certain criticisms; the mission of the Twelve; the confession of Christ's messiahship; the transfiguration; a prophecy of death — fall roughly into the order which Mark has made familiar. But the remainder, and all from about 9:45–18:31, can only be described as 'miscellaneous memories'.

All concern the public ministry of Jesus, and certain themes recur. A long journey may be the thread upon which isolated paragraphs are strung like pearls. Some sections seem to be paired, or grouped in threes, to provide a contrast, or to develop a theme. But these hints apart, the long middle section of Luke must be studied as miscellaneous notes on the life and words of Jesus. Remembering the notes of his journeys which Luke assembled in that 'travel diary', and his claim to have enquired among eye-witnesses and ministers of the word in order to follow all things accurately, such notes and jotted memories are just what we might expect. Where historical or logical settings of items were known, Luke would preserve them, but the separate reminiscences of individuals he met, of villages and homes he visited, would be noted and reproduced with no attempt at artificial arrangement. Luke was less concerned with historical sequence than with spiritual truth.

This is not guesswork; the vagueness of time, place, and connection of many paragraphs makes it clear.

> Beginning at 5:12 'When he was in one of the cities' the sequence runs, 'on one of those days . . . After this he went out and saw . . .' (where?) 'On a sabbath . . . On another sabbath . . . In these days . . . Soon afterward . . . Soon afterwards he went on . . . When a great crowd

came together . . . One day . . . Now it happened that as he was praying . . . He was praying in a certain place . . . Now he was casting out a demon . . . When the crowds were increasing . . . As he went away from there . . .' (from where?) 'In the meantime . . . He also said . . . At that very time . . .' (when?) 'Now he was teaching . . . One sabbath . . . He also said . . . And he said . . . And he told them a parable . . . He also told this parable . . . Now they were bringing even infants . . .'

So very often we would ask, 'Where, when, to whom, why?' or seek the connection between one paragraph and the next. If we think we have found answers, in contrasting paragraphs or continued themes, we must remember how easy it is to read our thoughts into Luke's words.

Luke's Gospel is obviously difficult to memorize or to recall. A survey or outline may help us to find our way, provided we do not let it prejudice our interpretation.

1:1	Preface

Backgrounds

1:5	The Baptist's background and conception
26	Background of Jesus; announcement to Mary; her response

Births and Acclaim

57	Of John
2:1	Of Jesus; angels, shepherds, Simeon, Anna

Public Appearances

39	Jesus visits the temple
3:1	Appearance of John
21	Appearance and baptism of Jesus; his genealogy

Christ's Ministry Begins

4:1	Alternative methods reviewed (temptation)
14	Manifesto at Nazareth
31	Capernaum inauguration; first miracles

Miscellaneous Memories

5:1	Call of Peter, James, John; 12: Leper and paralysed man healed; 27: Call of Levi; 33: Criticism — fasting
6:1	Criticism — sabbath; 12: Choice of the Twelve; 17: Growing fame; 20: Collected sayings — blessing and woe, love, judging others, inner goodness, two housebuilders

7:1   Two miracles; 18: Jesus on John; 36: The woman of the city
8:1   Increasing support; 4: The sower parable; 16: Light on a stand; 19: Christ's family defined; 22: Stilling a storm and a demoniac; 40: Healing a woman, raising a girl
9:1   Mission of the Twelve; 7: Herod's reaction; 10: Five thousand fed; 18: Confession of messiahship; 23: Saving and losing life; 28: The transfiguration; 37: The epileptic; 43: Prophecy of death; 46: Greatness and the child; 49: For or against?

More Miscellaneous Memories — Approaching Jerusalem
9:51 Inhospitable Samaritans; 57: Discipleship's demands
10:1 Mission of the seventy; 21: Jesus rejoices; 25: The good Samaritan; 38: Martha and Mary
11:1 Lesson on praying; 14: Accusation of devilry; 27: The ground of blessing; 29: Signs without, light and cleanness within; 42: Reproach of leaders
12:1 Fear and fearlessness; 13: Avarice and anxiety; 35: The watchful servants and faithful steward; 49: The divisive Christ; 54: Insight and sense
13.1 Calamity, repentance, and God's patience; 10: Sabbath work; 18: Mustard, leaven; 22: Strive to enter; 31: Herod and Jerusalem threaten
14:1 Healing on the sabbath; 7: Dining out; 25: Terms of discipleship
15:1 Why befriend sinners? — lost sheep, coin, son
16:1 Unscrupulous and faithful stewards; 16: The kingdom and the law; 18: On divorce; 19: Reversal of fortunes — parable of Lazarus
17:1 Sin, forgiveness and faith; 7: Unworthy servants; 11: The grateful leper; 20: The kingdom within; 22: The coming of the kingdom
18.1 God's sure vindication; 9: Two at prayer; 15: The kingdom of the childlike; 18: Salvation and riches; 31: Prophecy of death; 35: Healing of blind man
19:1 Zaccheus — money misused, used; 28: Jesus in Jerusalem

Beginning of the End
20:1 Challenge to Christ's authority
9   The vineyard of God
19   Traps set for Christ (taxes, resurrection)
41   Christ counter-attacks

In some ways, such an outline is disappointing, almost impossible to keep in mind. It is well at this point to read the Gospel straight through with the outline beside it. Such effort will certainly make the contents more familiar, and provide a check on the opinions expressed. Such reading may also throw some light, here and there, on passages not formerly noticed so carefully.

A Closer Look

It will be useful to consider briefly a few of the preliminary, background questions which attentive reading may raise, but which need not greatly affect our understanding of Luke's wider purpose. For example, Luke introduces Jesus by means of seven idyllic scenes, probably deliberately archaic in tone, and intensely Jewish in colouring. By these, he sets Jesus firmly within a human and domestic frame. For Luke's purpose, and his readers, this method has greater relevance than John's highly theological introduction, by the doctrine of the eternal Word and the wonder of incarnation. Instead, Luke will let the theological implications in the story emerge in the telling, but it soon becomes clear that Luke thought Jesus was more than human.

Luke on John the Baptist (Luke 1–3)

Luke affords to the Baptist a surprising prominence in the story, telling us much more than do the other evangelists of John's background, birth, and message, paying him warm tribute (3:18–20), repeating the high tribute paid by Jesus also (7:24–28), and noting Jesus' unfailing loyalty to John, although John had mistaken ideas about the ministry of the coming Messiah (20:3–8, 23:9, against 3:16–17, 7:18–19). Luke clearly regards John as preparing for Jesus, initiating a community of disciples (whom he taught to fast and to pray, 5:33, 11:1), all of whom had publicly expressed repentance, in the form of symbolic cleansing already familiar in Levitical rites, and later extended to converts from 'unclean' races in the rite of proselyte-baptism. In Luke's mind, it is sufficient, to explain Jesus' baptism at John's hands, that Jesus considered John and his movement was 'from heaven', and so carried God's authority (20:2–4). Jesus, indeed, applied to John the prophecy of Malachi 3:1, concerning the messenger to be sent before the face of the Lord (7:27, compare 1:17, 76, identified in Malachi 4:5–6 and Matthew 17:9–13 with the returned Elijah, though Luke does not name him).

By Luke's time, John was widely accepted in Judaism as the reawakening of divine prophecy in Israel, after at least two centuries of silence (note John's disciples at *Ephesus*, Acts 19:3). Luke therefore links Jesus closely with John, as a living sign of the new age of the Spirit, and as a strong and influential testimony to Jesus' messiahship.

Luke and Miracles

John's birth, like that of Jesus, would be miraculous in Luke's eyes. Miracles have become intellectually respectable since scientists took to performing them, but also much harder to define. Perhaps the best description at the present time would run, 'a miracle is an event of which the full explanation has not yet been published, and which science has not so far imitated'. Belief in the resurrection of Jesus makes any miracle credible, but not every Christian credulous. Whether any particular event was a miracle (in the older sense) depends upon its nature, and the evidence for it. Luke would probably assume, without a second thought, that God who made the world is not fettered by it but is free to act in any way consistent with his character and purpose.

The Virgin Birth

That Jesus was born of a virgin would be an article of faith, to Luke as to most Christians today. Our faith rests mainly upon Luke's testimony and the church's historic creed. Matthew also assumes that Jesus was virgin-born, offering no source for the information, but linking it directly with a verse in Isaiah which originally referred to a very different situation. On this subject, obviously, no test of personal Christian experience can turn reverent opinion into 'conviction', and while holding loyally to the church's faith for themselves, modern Christians may fairly acknowledge that some unanswerable questions arise. Why, for example, does Luke trace the genealogy of Jesus through Joseph? To talk of 'merely legal descent' from David would sound to Jewish critics like legal fiction (3:23–24 compare 2:48). And why was virgin birth necessary? Both Paul and John argue strongly for Christ's divinity without needing to mention a virgin birth; the epistle to the Hebrews emphasizes Christ's superiority to all others *and* his kinship with us, without mentioning virgin birth. The idea that a virgin birth 'cut off the entail of inherited sin' is nowhere advanced in scripture, and it assumes that such an entail is transmitted only through a father. Certainly, nothing in the manner of Christ's birth must be used to suggest that bisexual procreation is sinful, or that sex and marriage are not sacred, or divinely instituted. Beside such questions, which merely justify tolerance and charity in discussion, must be set the strong probability that Luke's informants included the circle around Mary, and quite possibly Mary herself, at Caesarea and Jerusalem. It could only be from some such intimate source that Luke obtained his detailed knowledge of Mary, and of the infancy and boyhood years.

Christ's Boyhood

Jesus would attain Bar-Mitzvah ('son of the Law') at 12–13 years of age, the threshold of manhood (girls were marriageable at 15). His father was charged to instruct him during the previous year, and further instruction by rabbis at open-air classes in the temple courtyard was part of the recognition ceremonies. Villagers journeyed together to such feasts, and it was easy to assume that the now grown lad would be among those of his own age. One day travelling homewards, missing Jesus at evening, one day returning, and finding him on the third day, explains 2:43. Luke avoids any impression of a child-prodigy putting the rabbis right (as some apocryphal stories suggest). 2:52 describes a gracious, attractive personality developing naturally; is a contrast intended with 1:80, where John appears a strong-willed 'lone wolf' lad?

Christ's Temptation

The temptation being private, the story must come from Jesus, and describe in his usual pictorial language a genuine, not a pretended, temptation. 'If you are the son of God . . .' (4:3, 9) argues from the assurance that came at his baptism (3:22), and confirms that the temptations represent alternative ways of attaining the messianic kingdom. We know that similar temptations as to method faced Jesus throughout his ministry, as indeed Luke suggests (4:13; compare respectively John 6:15, 26 after feeding five thousand; Luke 11:29–30; John 18:36, for violence was Satan's way to rule).

Demonology

The first of Luke's many exorcism-stories begins at 4:33. As in the Temptation, the existence of the devil and his kingdom in the world are assumed, with the power of his subordinate demons to cause physical, mental and moral harm, disease, and decay — even by a physician. Four to seven-and-a-half millions of these demons ('spirits' or perhaps fallen angels) were supposed to inhabit the upper air and wild, unclean places, usually invisible but assuming various shapes, and entering human personality when sin gave them opportunity. Satan headed grades of demon powers ('principalities, powers, world-rulers of this present darkness, spiritual hosts of wickedness', Ephesians 6:12). Most of the ancient world lived in perpetual fear of malignant demonic powers, ubiquitous as germs. Luke declared that Christ had overcome Satan, bound the strong one, watched Satan falling from heaven, and by superior power had delivered those bound or 'possessed' (4:1–13, 36, 41, 6:18, 8:2, 26–35, 10:18, 11:15–26, 13:16). The first evidence of Christian victory with Christ was the loss of all fear of demons; many would say that the final evidence of complete victory is disbelief in their existence. For modern Christians, a decision will rest on how far demonology is essential to the gospel story, since Jesus spoke in these terms; how far it is merely part of the first-century language in which Jesus had inevitably to speak in order to be understood, but no permanent element in Christian faith.

Jesus and the Crowds

Luke makes much of the crowds continually around Jesus (4:40, 42, 5:1, 15, 6:17, 8:4 'from town after town', 40 'waiting for him', 45, 9:11 'he welcomed them', 37, 11:29 'increasing', 12:1 'thousands . . . trod upon one another', 14, 14:25 'great multitudes', 19:37, 20:19, 21:38 'early in the morning'). In Luke, they do not appear to dwindle; even at the end Jesus walks in safety in daylight, because the authorities 'feared the people' if they attempted to arrest him (22:2).

It is an important element in Luke's story that Jesus' relationship with these crowds was relaxed and informal; he was a most popular teacher.

One of Christ's favourite teaching methods, especially prominent in Luke, was to pose questions, which involved the hearers in his theme and challenged their thought. There are some *ninety* questions put by Jesus in Luke's Gospel, of which *seventy* are substantial, stimulating, memorable 'texts' for further discussion. Unlike the Pharisees, Jesus was not didactic, but 'Socratic', an insatiable enquirer, evoking opinions, opening the mind to new ideas and judgements, and — very significantly — appealing to the common people's moral insight as the premise upon which to build further understanding (12:57). Hence Jesus' emphasis upon the necessity that a man's inner light shine clearly, and his inner eye be true (11:34–36). Sometimes, though, to the authorities and to his critics, Christ's questions were very provocative, and disconcerting (6:8–9, 7:24–26, 13:15–16, 14:3, 20:3–6, 41).

The crowds, on their part, were equally relaxed with Jesus. Individuals among them spoke up freely to ask questions or to prompt comment (9:57, 61, 10:25, 11:27, 45, 12:13, 13:1, 23, 14:15), or groups put concerted questions (17:20, 20:1–2). Sometimes members of the crowd actually protested at what Jesus said, 'heckling' his open-air teaching and obtaining immediate replies (19:25, 20:16).

Of Jesus' other attractive teaching-method, story-parables, Luke gives some nineteen examples. But he also preserves (in milder form than Mark's) a warning which suggests that the purpose of parables was to *hide* the truth (8:9–10). The point is that the real message of the parables is not always as obvious as the hearer supposes. He may, by hardness of heart, shallowness, or preoccupation, lose the seed of truth he received. He who has ears must therefore listen carefully (8:5–8). Those eager to learn, like the disciples now asking for explanation, are given the plain truth, which the careless listener misses. So parables sift their hearers.

Advantages of a Miscellany

A mere glance over the offered outline from 5:1 to 19:27 will confirm that great ingenuity is necessary to discover any thread of discourse or story linking the disparate items. We may ask, then, what has become of Luke's 'orderliness'? and the answer underlines one great advantage of Luke's method. He has retained, in a number of instances, the original setting of sayings and incidents, by not seeking to fit them into any pattern of teaching. It is obvious that Mark has brought together five stories illustrating opposition to Jesus, with the result that a decision to destroy him is reached as early as Mark 3:6. That suited Mark's purpose, but the five incidents did not occur at once, or so early. With the skill of a practised teacher, Matthew has arranged many sayings of Jesus into five great discourses on related themes (see *Matthew Lays It On The Line!*); a somewhat rambling 'sermon' on the mountainside, seven parables with commentary, two long chapters on the future, for example. And in Matthew 8–9, eleven great miracles, one after the other, almost without interruption. That is useful for teaching. Luke avoids systematizing, and as a result each incident or saying may be considered on its own, as Luke first learned it.

One very striking example concerns the Lord's prayer, which Matthew places within the 'Sermon on the Mount' amid three other sayings on prayer, in a section concerned with ostentatious piety. Luke says that when Jesus was praying in a certain place, as he ceased one of the disciples said to him, 'Lord, teach us to pray, as John taught his disciples'; to which Jesus responded with the simple pattern-prayer. It is not hard to decide which is likeliest to be the original setting of the lesson. (It solves nothing to suggest that Jesus could have given the pattern-prayer twice, since in that case neither Gospel tells the whole truth about it!)

A second very interesting example concerns the parable of the lost sheep. Matthew assembles several sayings on the relation of disciples to each other, their self-discipline, the handling of disputes, the need for a forgiving spirit among fellow-servants of the kingdom (Matthew 18). Into this context Matthew places the parable of the lost sheep, which becomes a lesson on caring for young converts, 'little ones who believe in me' but who may be tempted to sin or to be weak (Matthew 18:6–9, 12). The lost sheep is the erring church member, as the following verses make clear.

But Luke shows that the shepherd's selfless care for the lost sheep was first described in answer to the accusation of the self-righteous, evoked by Christ's success among the 'unchurched' — 'This man receives *sinners*, and eats with them!' (Luke 15:1–2). Repetition of the story by Jesus is not impossible; but it seems more probable that the treasured parable has been applied, in the church's reflection, to another situation. It is perfectly true that the same evangelistic care which the church shows towards outsiders must not be forgotten when sin occurs among her members.

The sayings about the narrow door, and the rejection of insincere claims, are given a much more realistic setting in Luke 13:22–27 than in Matthew 7:13–14, 21–23, in a public sermon at the outset of Christ's ministry. It must be added that sometimes the original setting or occasion of a saying or incident is lost, and Luke, too, can only list sayings which seem to have no inner connection, and which must be read as separate, unrelated utterances. The swift transition from understanding the time, to moral insight, to settling law-suits promptly, in 12:54–59, is an example; the coherence of 14:31–35 is hard to find; even more disjointed is 16:14–18; and it is a relief to suppose that

16:9–13 did not originally belong to the preceding parable (compare Matthew 6:24).

A second advantage of Luke's unstructured miscellany of gathered memories lies in his setting two or three items side by side to make a significant point silently. The stilling of the storm at sea is followed immediately by the stilling of the storm of madness in an unhinged mind. That interesting conjunction occurs also in Matthew and in Mark, and presumably is historically based. But the Samaritans' refusal of hospitality is followed by the warning that to follow the Son of man may mean having nowhere to lay one's head, only in Luke. And so is the linking of Jesus' refusal of outward 'signs' with the need for inward light and inward cleansing.

The accusation that Jesus exorcises demons by the devil's help, and the warning that exorcism alone is not enough unless divine possession follows, are separated in Matthew, but closely linked in Luke, adding weight to the argument. Three complementary sayings on fear, expounding fear which is healthy, fear which is weakening, are placed together in Luke 12:1, 4, 5, 11, but scattered in Matthew. Luke 12:13–34 impressively links avarice, anxiety, and the seeking of heavenly riches. Probably Jesus first grouped these thoughts, but Luke saw why, and preserved the connection. Matthew breaks them, and provides a very different setting (Mathew 6:25–33, 10–21).

In Luke 13:1–9 the stern call to repentance is beautifully balanced with the parable of divine patience. Three pieces of advice about banquets are fittingly brought together in 14:7–24, by Luke only. Alert reading will suggest other examples of Luke's contrasting or coupling items of information, sometimes less obviously, though care is needed not to invent examples. Did Luke deliberately set that awful judgement on the corrupter of children beside the call to forgive seven times any man who repents (17:1–4)? Was the story of the vineyard tenants who refused to pay their rental to God deliberately placed to introduce the challenge about paying tax-rental to Caesar and the demand 'Render . . . to God the things that are God's'?

That Long Journey

'A long journey may be the thread on which isolated paragraphs are strung like pearls': the possibility was mentioned earlier, and deserves a little more attention. The suggestion arises from certain phrases read consecutively in the order in which Luke uses them, between 9:51 and 19:45:

> 'When the days drew near for him to be received up, he set his face to go to Jerusalem. And he sent messengers ahead of him . . . His face was set toward Jerusalem . . . They went on to another village . . . As they were going along the road . . . He sent them on ahead . . . into every town and place where he himself was about to come . . . Now as they went on

their way he entered a village . . . He went on his way through towns and villages, teaching, and journeying toward Jerusalem . . . Some Pharisees came and said to him, "Get away from here . . ." . . . "I must go on my way today and tomorrow and the day following . . ." And great multitudes accompanied him . . . On the way to Jerusalem he was passing along between Samaria and Galilee . . . And taking the Twelve he said to them, "Behold, we are going up to Jerusalem . . ." . . . As he drew near to Jericho . . . He entered Jericho and was passing through . . . The way was near to Jerusalem . . . He went on ahead, going up to Jerusalem . . . When he drew near to Bethphage and Bethany . . . As he was now drawing near, at the descent of the mount of Olives . . . And when he drew near and saw the city . . . And he entered the temple . . .'
(9:51–53, 56–57, 10:1, 38, 13:22, 31, 33, 14:25, 17:11, 18:31, 35, 19:1, 11, 28–29, 37, 41, 45)

This impression of a continuous journey can hardly be accidental. But it is not without difficulties. According to 9:52, Jesus travelled through Samaria, but at 19:1 he passes through Jericho, which was not on the direct road through Samaria, but on the road east of Jordan which Jews preferred to use. In 10:38, Jesus has reached Bethany, near Jerusalem, but at 17:11 he is still on the border between Galilee and Samaria. The crowds mentioned, the several synagogue services, the hostility of Herod, all seem to belong to days in Galilee, not Samaria or Perea (east of Jordan). And so very much seems to have occurred on this journey of about 160 kilometres (100 miles); Luke mentions some sixty incidents or speeches.

Certainly Jesus travelled the roads north and south several times; and much occurred on his journeys. It may be Luke knew of many such incidents 'on the road', and did not intend them to be understood as happening on the *same* journey. One effect of the 'eventful journey' impression is to heighten again and again the sense of impending danger, as he drew nearer and nearer to the city. There is no reason why Luke should not have intended that effect, except that it seems to depart somewhat from his usual unstructured method.

In truth, the meaning of this 'journey' framework (if that is what it is) for these particular incidents, is open to any reverent guess. It recalls the 'travel diary' used in *Acts*. It recalls too Luke's apparent fondness for journeys — Mary's to Elizabeth, the shepherds to Bethlehem, Joseph and Mary homewards without Jesus, the journey to Emmaus, the journeys of Philip and Peter, the extended travelogues of Paul, the voyage to Rome, the journey of the gospel from Jerusalem to the end of the earth.

Luke's own Christian life had ushered him into considerable globetrotting, taking in Macedonia, Asia Minor, Syria, Palestine, Malta, and Italy; it was an adventure with Christ. One of the first names for Christianity was 'the Way', as Luke himself three times records (Acts 9:2, 19:9, 23). Did he, like Bunyan, conceive of Christian life itself as essentially a pilgrimage, a moving ever onwards, with Christ?

There is no harm in such guesses. Others are less plausible. That for Luke, all the place-names used were symbols of theological ideas, for example. Thus the journey Luke described was from the Baptist's position (repentance) at Jordan to 'the teaching position' (Galilee), via the 'prayer position' (the mountains), and on to the 'salvation position' (Calvary) — the necessary movement of Christian faith. How astonished Luke would be! It has been suggested, too, that the real journey that Luke describes was that from Bethlehem to Rome, in two travelogues.

With so skilled an author, who chose so carefully the opening scene of his account of Christ's ministry — the 'manifesto' sermon at Nazareth — we might expect that the closing scene will be just as carefully chosen, to summarize and underline the main message of the Gospel. And we are not disappointed. It had to be a resurrection story, but it is superbly fitting that it should be one which only Luke has saved for us. It is of another journey — the road to Emmaus. For certainly the Emmaus incident is a paradigm or pattern of the Christian life: walking homewards, at the end of the day, out of bewilderment, disappointment, grief, and doubt, to which even Jesus is a 'stranger', through heart-burning illumination and understanding, to recognition in the breaking of bread. Then the swift return to share their joy with others, and a new corporate experience of Christ's presence, promise, and commission.

There the Gospel had to finish. That's it, that's the whole point; that is what it is all about. Life becomes a sponsored walk beside the risen Christ, with home and joy at the end.

CHAPTER 6

Luke's Workmanship

Coming from a Gentile background into an already existing church, Luke had to learn from those who were in Christ before him the common tradition about Jesus, and what it meant for salvation. He found Christians ever ready to talk about 'the Lord, Jesus', to share information, insights, memories, the Lord's sayings, things repeated and discussed in Christian worship or in household fellowship, the origin and meaning of Christian baptism, the story behind the Lord's supper, what Jesus had said about paying taxes, about marriage, the sabbath, love, children, his death, his coming again, and so much more. For thirty or forty years this collective memory of Jesus was circulated and handed down to new converts *by word of mouth*, and therefore with minor variations. Outside Palestine it was repeated no longer in Aramaic but translated, as each teacher was able, into Greek.

We know that to aid memories, patterns became established, both of evangelistic preaching and of convert-training. The Hebrew scriptures, with Christian explanations, would be shared by most Christian groups. Luke had first to absorb this corporate oral tradition about Jesus and the Christian 'Way', as the fountain and nourishment of his own discipleship, and the prerequisite of all that he was to contribute.

Luke and the Common Tradition

By the sixties of the first century, the passing of the first eye-witnesses and the receding of the advent hope quickened a desire to record the first generation's memories. Luke knew that many had undertaken to compile narratives, and appears to have read some of them, and felt that they could be improved upon. What happened to these 'many' attempts we do not know, but one such early narrative does survive — the Gospel of Mark.

Much of what Luke has to tell he shares with Mark. Out of Mark's 661 verses, Luke repeats the *content* of some 330/350 (it is difficult to count exactly when the length of verses in the two books varies widely). This of course we would expect, since they tell the same story. The unexpected feature of this overlapping is that Luke reproduces well over half of Mark's actual *words*, and (where he takes from Mark) much of Mark's *order* also. Often, where Luke departs from Mark's words (in telling the same story), or from Mark's order of items, we can see why, especially where he 'edits' Mark to improve vocabulary, grammar, or clarity. Facts like these leave little doubt that Luke made use of the Gospel of Mark.

Obviously, Matthew and Luke tell more than Mark does, and often overlap each other. Surprisingly, we find very much the same is true of this overlapping, also. In some 200/250 verses where Matthew and Luke are telling of the same things, yet did not borrow from Mark, many of the same words and much the same order occur. This similarity is too close for coincidence; and yet the information is so differently used, and the total result so different, that it is hard to believe that either copied from the other. The simplest explanation is that both Matthew and Luke obtained this shared information from another source, each using and editing it as he wished.

What that other source might be it is hard to decide. The 200/250 verses concerned are almost entirely sayings of Jesus — parables, epigrams, lessons, beatitudes; only one incident is included. We may think of it therefore as the 'Sayings source', and be grateful for what it adds to our knowledge of the teaching of Jesus. Some have stressed how similar are these verses in Matthew and Luke, and think they must come from some pamphlet or small book. Others point to the differences in Matthew's and Luke's use of them, and think the information was committed to memory. A largely non-literary society has to cultivate remarkable memory-power, and a teaching system based on remembering, not writing notes. In addition, much of Jesus' teaching is cast deliberately into easily remembered picturesque, poetic, and rhythmic form. It may well be therefore that Luke drew upon a memorized pattern, if not a written one, preserving some of Jesus' teaching, to supplement his own collected notes of what Jesus had taught.

For Luke did more than *absorb* and *record* information already circulating in the churches. He made his own enquiries of the people he met, and the villages and homes he visited, at Caesarea, Jerusalem, and elsewhere. So he greatly *amplified* our knowledge of Jesus, and with some of the most precious memories we possess, which only Luke recaptured. The parables of the good Samaritan, the lost coin, the prodigal son, the rich man and Lazarus, the rich fool, the embezzling steward, the unjust judge, the Pharisee and the tax collector, the barren tree, the two debtors, and the friend at midnight, would all have been lost for ever but for Luke's researches.

So would the story of the catch of fish at Peter's call, the miracle at Nain, the releasing of the bowed woman, the healing of dropsy, the cure of ten lepers, and of a right ear. But for Luke we would have missed the story of the shepherds at Bethlehem, the accounts of John's birth and of his preaching, almost all we know of Mary of Nazareth and her response to

God's call, the presentation of Christ in the temple, the boyhood visit to Jerusalem, the full account of Jesus' visit to Nazareth, and the story of the repentant woman in the house of Simon. We would have lost also the sayings on 'repent or perish', and humility, the stories of Zaccheus, Jesus before Herod, the dying thief, the final prayer of Jesus, and the walk to Emmaus. This is a remarkable list of the debts we owe to Luke's diligent enquiries; it is difficult to imagine the gospel story without these sayings and incidents.

Luke's Skill

Besides inheriting, recording, and amplifying the information about Jesus already available, Luke has fashioned all into a smoothly connected account, with charm, persuasiveness, and very clear purpose. Attention has already been drawn to the beautiful Hebrew poems that enrich chapters 1–2. If Luke himself composed them, a Gentile used to worshipping in Greek, but (in the Magnificat) using the ancient Hebrew Song of Hannah as his model, then Luke had something of genius. If Luke learned them from Mary, then his appreciation of them, and his skill in using them so effectively to create the atmosphere of devotion into which Jesus and John were born, must still rank him high among Bible writers. Luke's mastery of Greek, his beauty of style, his ability to make significant points silently by placing items side by side, and his retaining of original contexts and connections, all add to our appreciation of Luke as an author.

The same independence of mind which saved Luke from merely echoing Paul is manifest again in his handling of the information that came to him. As we would expect, and as Matthew reveals, most of the tradition about Jesus had been handed down in Jewish and messianic terms, coloured by the contention with a self-righteous, legalist, and nationalist outlook, and the slow break with Judaism. Even Mark, though writing for the Roman church, retains something of this Jewish tone and colour, while concentrating upon the conflicts in which Jesus became engaged. But Luke's special audience would need, and appreciate, neither aspect of the story. Luke presents his own picture of Jesus, with his own emphasis, not contradicting the accepted tradition but selecting and underlining different aspects, because he wrote for a different readership. Unless we realize the immense value, and courage, of this procedure, we miss the greatness of Luke's achievement.

Respect for Luke's careful workmanship increases further if we raise, reverently, certain puzzling questions and seek with due caution for reasonable answers. There is no real doubt that Luke used *Mark*; but why only about *half* of Mark's Gospel? and why in such an odd manner? Luke begins without anything from Mark, since Mark says nothing of Jesus' childhood and youth. Then Luke borrows from Mark for a little, but ·

proceeds without his help. Then he uses *Mark* again, and so on, four or five times. Next he combines something from *Mark* with his own researches; and then for nearly nine chapters (9:51–18:14) he ignores *Mark* altogether. He returns to combining *Mark* with his own original material, and finally chooses his own ending, quite different from *Mark*. All this rests, of course, upon very detailed comparison of the two Gospels in Greek.

Obviously Luke is not following *Mark* as a guide. And he never combines information from *Mark* with that from the 'Sayings source'. Further, it is contended that, if we read straight through the passages where Luke does not borrow anything from *Mark* (3:1 to 4:30, 5:1–11, 6:12 to 8:3, 9:51 to 18:14, 19:1–28, 37–44, 47–48, 22:14 to 24:53), subtracting, so to speak, *Mark's* information from *Luke*, we shall find that it reads reasonably smoothly, as a shorter story of Jesus, though not an adequate Gospel, as Luke himself probably realized.

For the suggestion is that Luke first sketched his Gospel from his own researches and the 'Sayings source'; later he supplemented that 'early draft' from Mark's account, when a copy reached him. Thus parts of his own 'early draft' remained unchanged, and parts were combined with what *Mark* supplied, while some passages not previously in the 'early draft' at all were now added. That would explain (*a*) the strange use of *Mark's* information only at scattered places in Luke's Gospel, in 'patches'; (*b*) why Luke's Gospel, with *Mark's* contribution removed, still reads fairly smoothly; (*c*) the puzzling, elaborate date suddenly introduced at 3:1, when the story is well on its way (3:1 would, on this explanation, be the actual beginning of Luke's 'early draft'); (*d*) the odd introduction of the Baptist in 3:2 as 'John the son of Zechariah' as though we had not already been told of his parentage, birth, and background; and (*e*) the giving of Christ's genealogy, not as in Matthew at Christ's birth, but after his baptism — which would be the first mention of Christ's name in the supposed 'early draft'.

This theory about Luke's procedure has been debated with great ability and zeal on both sides for over fifty years, which shows that it has never been proved — or disproved. If it is ever established, we shall possess another very early source for the life of Jesus, beside the 'Sayings' and Mark's Gospel, namely Luke's 'early draft'. We would also receive some help, if the theory could be proved, with a puzzling contradiction about the date when Luke wrote.

For, to be of any use, the *Acts* defence of Christianity, reciting Paul's acquittals, must have been written before Paul's death. The Gospel we have was written before *Acts* (Acts 1:1), giving us the sequence, Gospel, *Acts* defending Paul, Paul's death. But this will not do. For the Gospel borrows from *Mark*, and *Mark* was written *after* Paul's death. The contradiction would be resolved if we could be persuaded that Luke wrote an 'early draft' of his Gospel, without *Mark*, and later supplemented it from *Mark*. The sequence would then be (*a*) Luke's first draft, written perhaps while he was in Palestine, at Caesarea, or while Paul awaited trial at Rome; (*b*) *Acts*, defending Christianity and especially Paul, written next, in time to help Paul; (*c*) Paul's death; (*d*) Luke, at Rome, comes upon Mark's Gospel, and recognizing the insufficiency of his own brief 'early draft', supplements it from *Mark*, probably adding at the same time the stories of the Infancy (Luke 1–2).

It is well that all this speculation does not greatly affect either the interpretation or the appreciation of the Gospel. The Gospel was certainly known by the middle of the second century, and nothing in it conflicts with a date soon after Mark wrote, which places *Luke* around AD 70 or 80. Where Luke wrote is equally doubtful. Alexandria, Greece, Rome, all have defenders. But whenever, and wherever Luke did his final composing, his careful workmanship has served succeeding generations in every land, to their immeasurable enrichment.

Luke's Historical Veracity

Luke's claim, to have followed all things accurately to produce an orderly account, raises inevitably the question of his reliability as an historian, though the enquiry concerns *Acts* more than the Gospel. Nothing resembling impartial 'scientific' history must be expected in the ancient world, any more than today. All history writing involves selection, relation, assessment and explanation of facts, each a subjective process from which the motives and prejudices of the historian cannot be eliminated. Ancient historians confessed to studying history to ensure that virtues were not ignored and wickedness, from the exposure of its consequences, was dreaded; or, to exhibit the causes of disastrous events, so avoiding their repetition. Luke wrote, as a Christian, the case for Christianity, and therefore 'theological history', or history with a meaning.

On the other hand, Luke means his history to be taken seriously, and not as history made to conform to a theory. By the time he wrote, the gnostic tendency to dissolve the gospel story into mere symbols of abstract, timeless truths, was deeply troubling the church (compare 1 John 1:1–3, 4:2–3). Luke insists that what he records was actually 'accomplished among us' (Luke 1:1), and 'not done in a corner' (Acts 26:26), or at some indeterminate time (Luke 2:2, 3:1–2). Yet personal conviction and commitment need not make the work dishonest, but only more careful. A defence that can be demonstrated to be false is worse than useless, it incriminates.

Many would simply assume Luke's accuracy, as an act of Christian faith in divine inspiration. That is defensible, but Luke himself makes no such claim, as an Old Testament prophet might have done. We must recall his exceptional qualifications again — the years with Paul; the travel from Macedonia to Palestine, and then to Rome, meeting Christian groups constantly, including many eye-witnesses and leaders of the apostolic church in Jerusalem and elsewhere; the sources available to him; his own spiritual experience and personal gifts and temperament.

General marks of fidelity to truth may be seen in Luke's respect for awkward facts, like the slowness of the disciples to understand Jesus, and their quarrelsomeness towards the end; the denial of Jesus by Peter, spite of warning; the betrayal of Jesus by one of his own choosing; the disciples' unbelief in the resurrection, and the eating of fish by the risen Lord. Similarly, Luke does not omit or gloss the failures of the church — the dissension over distribution of alms; the contention between Paul and Barnabas; the dishonesty of Ananias and Sapphira; the division in the church over welcoming the Gentiles. In making out a case it would be so easy to pass over, or to excuse, regrettable details. And not even Luke's joyous optimism is allowed to soften the realistic description of the high cost of discipleship, or the agony of Jesus.

On a few debated details, especially Luke's use of official titles in *Acts*, Luke has been vindicated by linguistic and archaeological research. It used to be said that he had only a 'tourist's' knowledge of Palestine, but that is exactly what he was. He knew that the Roman headquarters were at Caesarea, Olivet a sabbath day's journey from Jerusalem, Emmaus about sixty stadia; he was acquainted with the Beautiful Gate, and Solomon's colonnade, in the temple, and with the internal stairway up to the tower of Antonia.

Two statements in the Gospel have occasioned more debate. Luke says that Lysanias was tetrarch of Abilene when the Baptist's ministry began, whereas Josephus the Jewish historian records the death of Lysanias about 35 BC. A later reference by Josephus, an inscription, a coin, and certain other allusions, seem to prove there was a second Lysanias, possibly son of the first, to whom Luke refers.

The reference in Luke 11:51 to 'the blood of Zechariah, who perished between the altar and the sanctuary' has also caused some discussion. It was assumed that Luke was speaking of Zechariah son of Barachiah, who was martyred in the temple in AD 68. Matthew does indeed give the name in this form (Matthew 23:35), and we have to accept that either Jesus did not utter the words — or he made a most unusual prediction, including a name, of someone to be murdered over thirty years later. Or some mistake has arisen in Matthew's text. For a careful comparison of Luke 11:51 with 2 Chronicles

24:20–22 leaves little doubt that Jesus was referring to the death of Zechariah son of Jehoiada, citing his dying words (in Hebrew, 'May the Lord *require* it . . .'). Since 2 Chronicles was the closing book of the Hebrew Bible, Jesus was citing the first and last examples of martyrdom in the Old Testament. Luke is thus right, though in fact the whole discussion arose because it was *assumed* he meant what Matthew said; Luke himself does not give the father's name!

On one detail it may have to be conceded that even Luke's historical conscience has nodded. Jesus could not be born in the reign of Herod the Great (died 4 BC) *and* at the time when Quirinius was 'governor' of Syria (AD 6–9). A somewhat battered inscription (found at Tivoli in 1764) is thought to show that Quirinius held an emergency military command in Syria about the required date, a command for which (it is suggested) Luke's Greek word might represent the Latin 'legatus' in its military rather than its civil sense. If so, Luke presumably mentions Quirinius as officer in charge of the politically provocative census. Here are too many uncertainties; Luke may have been merely misinformed. Protracted discussion has so far proved inconclusive.

Nevertheless, our conclusion must be that Luke is as careful a historian as he is expert as an author. For the special task of bringing the story and the message of Christ to a new and critical audience, God had chosen a well-tuned instrument of exceptional ability and devotion.

CHAPTER 7

Luke's Kingdom

At first sight it is surprising that Luke should mention 'the kingdom' some thirty-six times, and the related idea of Jesus' Davidic descent another six times, when writing for Romans of high rank. Doubtless he wished to keep faithfully to historic fact, and the message of Jesus certainly was first couched in messianic terms. Possibly any theme touching upon Statecraft would interest his audience. Yet it seems provocative, and even dangerous, to say so much about Christ's 'kingdom', remembering the Jews' rebellious reputation in Roman eyes. Without care, that topic alone could suffice to alienate Roman sympathy.

A Delicate Subject

Luke is in fact extremely careful. At the very first mention of Jesus' inheriting the throne of his father David, the idea is removed at once from all possibility of political or seditious interpretation. For it is as Son of the Most High that Jesus receives the throne, as the gift of the Lord God; he is to reign over the house of Jacob, 'and of his kingdom there will be no end'. This is the message of an angel (1:32–33). Thus the essentially religious nature of the kingdom is clear from the start, as are its divine origin, and timeless quality.

Similarly, the second reference to the thought of Christ as king shows him deliberately refusing 'all the kingdoms of the world' at the offer by the devil. There is no mistaking the meaning of that renunciation, for Luke's aristocratic readers. And this is confirmed by Luke's constant use of the phrase 'kingdom *of God*' (thirty times). However powerful Caesar's empire was, it could not be called that, or a rival to it. At the launching of this 'Messiah's' ministry, his manifesto was 'good news', not a battle cry, and nothing in the ensuing fifty years suggested that Jesus had intended to arouse sedition.

Besides, Luke emphasizes significantly that the kingdom Christ inaugurates comes by preaching. 'I must preach the good news of the kingdom of God . . . He went on through cities and villages preaching and bringing the good news of the kingdom of God . . . He sent them out to preach the kingdom of God . . . Leave the dead to bury the dead; but as for you, Go and proclaim the kingdom of God.' This preaching of the kingdom ends the period of the law and the prophets and marks the dawn of the kingdom's time, with the eager pressing into it (16:16). Preaching also fixes clearly the nature of the kingdom, for preaching is neither armed revolt nor violent uprising.

Moreover, the 'preaching' suggests a spreading of ideas, a cultivation of moral and mental qualities which the divine kingdom demands. Childlikeness for example, 'for to such belongs the kingdom of God', and whoever does not receive the kingdom with childlike receptiveness shall not enter it (18:16–17); or the acceptance of poverty, for entrance is especially hard for the rich and self-sufficient. The question of 'fitness' is raised, for 'no one who puts his hand to the plough and looks back is fit for the kingdom of God' (9:26). Men must learn its secret (8:10, probably the inner rule of God); must seek it as a first priority (12:31), even at the cost of family joys (18:29), and pray for its coming (11:2).

Already the age of the Spirit has dawned in Jesus; the powerful deeds and unanswerable words of Jesus *are* the kingdom of God already in operation among men. The kingdom is 'near', both in time and in accessibility, because Jesus is here. The power of Satan and his kingdom have already been broken, as Christ's repeated exorcisms show (see 4:6, 11:18, 13:16 with 11:20–22, 8:30–31, etc.). From now on, the slow, sure spread of this spiritual ideal of life divinely ruled will resemble the amazing development of the large shrub from the infinitesimal mustard seed; or the permeation of the heavy dough of society by the fermenting example, principles, and vision of Jesus (13:18, 20).

There is nothing here to trouble Roman patriotism. In the last analysis, 'the kingdom of God is not coming with signs to be observed', for the kingdom 'is in the midst of you' already, unobserved, a hidden yet powerful energy and ideal within society, and in that sense 'within you', too, as the motive force of individual lives. This was said to Pharisees who, holding a very different concept of the kingdom, asked when it was coming (17:20–21). Others 'who supposed that the kingdom of God was to appear immediately', were told the parable of the pounds concerning the interval of personal endeavour that must first be faithfully served (19:11–27).

Those (both Jews and Christians) who had expected an imminent personal 'arrival' of Messiah had already been disappointed, by the time Luke wrote, and he shows how Jesus warned that the 'fulfilment' of the kingdom would take time. But disciples need not fear, for it is the Father's good pleasure to 'give the kingdom' in his own time (12:32). Some in that generation would live to see the kingdom of God (9:27); those who (like Joseph of Arimathea) 'looked for' the kingdom of God would not be disappointed. Indeed, some were already seeing it, as the 'good news' of the Nazareth manifesto suggested. The disciples were to announce that 'the kingdom of God has come upon' their hearers; even if they reject it, people must know that 'it has come near' (10:9, 11).

But the kingdom is not yet 'fulfilled'. A time is coming when many will see patriarchs, prophets and aliens sitting in the kingdom and themselves shut out (13:28–29). There will be indications, like the natural signs of approaching summer, by which the vigilant will know that the kingdom of God is near (21:31). Meanwhile Jesus declines to eat or drink Passover bread and wine again until 'it is fulfilled in the kingdom of God . . . until the kingdom of God comes . . .'; then the disciples too will sit at his table in his kingdom (22:16, 18, 30). At the very last, as the dying thief asks to be remembered when Christ comes in his 'kingly power' (Greek, 'kingdom'), he is told '. . . Today you will be with me in Paradise' (23:43), a further hint of the timeless, extra-terrestrial frontiers of the kingdom.

In Luke's presentation, the older messianic hope, with its excited anticipation of the inbreaking of the divine order with signs and wonders to deliver Israel, has been transmuted into an idealist vision of good becoming triumphant, and the steady permeation of society by Christian ideals and invasive energies. This process has already begun, in Jesus' ministry and the preaching of the disciples; it has yet to reach its fulfilment in God's good time. For individuals, devotedly living under God's rule, the kingdom has come.

Nevertheless, Luke retains some of the older, vivid language about coming events. 'In his day' the Son of man will be like the lightning which lights the sky from one side to another, not in its suddenness but its ubiquity, so that rumours like 'He is here! he is there!' should be ignored (17:24). Again, 'There will be signs in sun, moon, stars . . . distress of nations . . . fainting . . . fear . . . foreboding . . . the powers of the heavens will be shaken and then they will see the Son of man coming in a cloud with power and great glory . . . Look up . . . your redemption is drawing near . . . But take heed lest . . . that day come like a snare . . . Watch at all times, praying that you may have strength . . . to stand before the Son of man' (21:25–28, 34–38).

These sayings closely resemble some of those in Matthew 24:29–51, where Jesus answers *two* questions, one about the destruction of the city and temple, the other about 'the sign of your coming and the close of the age'. By omitting the second question (compare Luke 21:7 with Matthew 24:3) Luke has telescoped the two events (fall of Jerusalem, 21:20–24; end of the age and coming of the Son of man, 25–28, 34–36). In Matthew the lesson of the fig tree concerns the coming of the Son of man; in Luke it refers to the nearness of the kingdom of God. Thus Luke's dramatic, eschatological language describes the final consummation of the age, when Christ's kingdom shall be fully and finally established in power.

In Luke's view, the kingdom of God has come for believing individuals; it is coming for society; it has yet to come in power over all mankind. This 'transmuted' hope of the kingdom has left Davidic messianism far behind. The Baptist's father had spoken of the link of the new age with 'the house of David', and Jewish Christians undoubtedly treasured the thought that Jesus was literally 'of the house and lineage of David', as prophets had said Messiah would be. Jesus himself (says Luke, 18:35–42) had publicly accepted the title 'son of David' from the lips of a blind man at Jericho. But in Hebrew phrase, 'son of . . .' implied more than genetic descent; it connoted likeness of character, role, and purpose (6:35, 'son of the Most High' in loving all men; compare 'son of peace', 'son of encouragement', 'son of the devil'). 'Son of David' had thus an imperialist, militarist implication, based upon David's massive and wide-ranging victories, and his reputation as a war leader.

Jesus therefore raised the question, how far the Messiah could truthfully be said to be 'son of David'? David himself had called the Messiah 'Lord', acknowledging an infinite difference between them; how then could Messiah be David's 'son', sharing identity and likeness (20:41–44)? Matthew makes the implication plainer, by preserving Christ's preliminary questions, 'What do you think of the Christ? Whose son is he?' — that is, what sort of Christ is he (Matthew 22:41–45)?

Thus both the king and the kingdom are of another kind than that anticipated in the Davidic hope, and offered to Jesus in his temptation. Luke's Messiah is neither militaristic, nor destined for earthly domination and glory; he is a *servant*, of God, and of sinful suffering humanity. Two aspects of this changed perspective deeply concerned Luke's readers.

A Universal Kingdom

The proud nationalism which had come to dominate the messianic hope, and which Gentiles sharply resented and derided, was now eliminated. Luke still uses certain terms which recall the Jewish origin of the idea of a kingdom of God, the word 'kingdom' itself, with its implication of monarchy, which Rome hated, and phrases like 'throne of David', 'house of Jacob', 'twelve tribes' (1:33, 22:30). But Luke transcends them. The *world* is in view, since Jesus reinterpreted the kingdom-idea. The kingdom is inter-racial, and Jesus himself is son not only of David but *of Adam* (3:38), and so belongs to all mankind. The kingdom of God is for Romans, too!

The Roman empire was a multi-racial, multi-national agglomeration of peoples, and the unifying of many races under one discipline and rule was a live issue, and a prolonged preoccupation, for leaders of Roman society. Luke would certainly have his readers' attention, as he demonstrated the extension of God's kingdom to Gentiles. *Acts* parallels the church's geographical expansion with a mental expansion of vision, as events and the Spirit prised open the church's mind to the wider world. But the beginning of that process, and the foundation of that argument, are in the Gospel. In both books Luke insists that Christ is a light to lighten the Gentiles (Luke 2:31–32, Acts 13:47, citing Isaiah 49:6), because this truth was as important to Luke himself, a foreigner admitted by Jesus to the people of God, as to his readers.

As the Gospel opens with this promise, so it closes with the divine purpose that salvation shall be preached in Christ's name 'to all nations' (24:47). Citing Isaiah's prevision of the voice crying in the wilderness, Luke (alone) carries the quotation forward to include the promise that 'all flesh shall see the salvation of God' (3:6). In the Nazareth sermon, seemingly without need, Jesus introduced highly provocative references to the foreign (Sidonian) widow to whom God turned to nourish his prophet Elijah, when 'there were many widows in Israel'; and to the healing of the Syrian, Naaman, from leprosy, when there were lepers enough in Israel. That the congregation was 'filled with wrath' is scarcely surprising, though we may be surprised that, so early, Jesus should throw down this particular gauntlet of geographical and ethnic universalism.

But the unexpected theme is sustained. Samaritans were among the most despised foreigners, yet, in *Luke*, Jesus avoids a clash with a hostile Samaritan village which refused him hospitality (9:51–56); he draws special attention to one leper grateful for healing — 'this foreigner' a Samaritan; he deliberately sharpens the lesson on loving one's neighbour by making his example a good Samaritan. Only Luke preserves the Jews' favourable description of one Gentile, 'He is worthy . . . for he loves our nation, and he built us our synagogue'; and only Luke adds to the foreigners from north and south who will sit at table with the patriarchs in the kingdom of God, others who will come from east and west (13:28–29, contrast Matthew 8:11–12).

In view of Luke's constant interest in the alien, and in the ostracized tax-servants of the empire, it is tempting to look for further indications, which considered alone might be unconvincing. 'The times of the Gentiles' (21:24) may suggest that Gentiles, too, had their allotted place in God's plan of history (compare Acts 17:26). Where Matthew says that the king's servants were commanded to go 'to the thoroughfares' to find guests for his banquet, Luke adds 'and hedges' (14:23). Amid so many of Jesus' sayings on prayer which Luke preserved, he does not record the words, 'Do not heap up empty phrases as the Gentiles do' (Matthew 6:7); nor does he record the hesitation of Jesus to perform a miracle for a Syro-Phoenician mother (Matthew 15:21–28, Mark 7:24–30). On the other hand, Luke alone records (ch 10) a mission by seventy (or seventy-two, the text is uncertain) to the towns and villages of Galilee, of which the most probable explanation is that it 'symbolizes' — or anticipates — the outreach of the gospel to the seventy (or seventy-two) nations that rabbis expounding Genesis 10, believed to comprise the whole world.

It is strange that this mission is mentioned nowhere else. That the instructions given should closely resemble those given to the Twelve on their mission is natural, the circumstances being so similar. That 22:35 — 'When I sent you out . . . lacked you anything? — is spoken to the Twelve but echoes 10:4, spoken to the seventy, gives one pause. Some suppose Luke to have received two accounts of the *same* mission; others, that he has read back into Christ's lifetime the apostolic mission to the world; and others guess that he constructed the story to symbolize something. If an intended parallel between Jesus and Moses were clear in the Gospel, we might agree that Jesus (like Moses) shared his burden with seventy (or seventy-two, Numbers 11:16–17, 24, 29), though the explanation seems far-fetched. The rabbis' count of seventy nations in the world according to Genesis 10 rests upon the Hebrew version; the Greek version yielded seventy-two. The fact that the text of Luke varies between the same two figures supports the suspicion that someone, if only a copyist of Luke, saw the mission of the seventy as a mission to all nations.

Whatever we make of these less obvious examples, Luke certainly shared all Paul's universalism, without Paul's phraseology, or his arguments about Jewish law and election. Matthew still recorded the gospel story in Jewish terms, and preserved a saying in which the Jews' privileged position as 'children' was contrasted with that of the Gentile 'dogs' (Matthew 15:26–27). John later assumes a Greek constituency for his Gospel, and to some extent addresses himself to it. Luke expounds the good news of the kingdom as a hope and a programme for the world; the kingdom of God is not for one exclusive race, or colour of skin, or sort of people, but for 'all peoples'. Luke admits that the original disciples were slow to grasp this truth, still asking the risen Christ 'Will you at this time restore the kingdom *to Israel*?' But Christ's answer sends them to 'the end of the earth'.

Yet Luke is no syncretist; he would never agree to 'let other races have their own religion if they are happy with it'. He believed that the prayers and almsgiving of a pious pagan were remembered by God (Acts 10:31), and that 'God shows no partiality, but in every nation any one who fears him and does what is right is acceptable to him' (Acts 10:34–35). But he had no doubt, either, that good pagans like Cornelius needed to hear the gospel of Christ (Acts 10:32, 36–43), or that 'there is salvation in no one else, for there is no other name under heaven given among men by which we must be saved' (Acts 4:12).

So too in the Gospel, Jesus is central and essential to the inter-racial, world-wide kingdom. Jesus is God's agent in its establishment, the supreme example and exponent of what it means in practice to live under the divine rule. Christianity would fulfil what was best in paganism, even as it did what was best in Judaism, but in the last resort its truth and power were independent of both, emanating solely from Christ. He was the divine king. His kingdom offered to the Roman world a unity and social cohesiveness that could yet make the whole world one.

A Kingdom of Peace

The other aspect of the changed perspective in which Luke sets the Davidic-messianic hope of a divine kingdom, is its peaceable aim. For a century or so, Palestine had been a problem province of the empire, and the Jews a turbulent, almost ungovernable people. The party which inherited the tenacity of the Maccabeans in defending Jewish faith, customs and partial independence, had in later years become increasingly militarist and battle-hungry. Their determination, and guerrilla tactics, had been a sore thorn in the side of Rome up to and after the fall of Jerusalem, until at Masada a thousand of these 'Zealots' had committed suicide rather than surrender to the Roman legions. Any new movement out of Palestine, talking of Messiah and a kingdom, would be bound to arouse apprehension in Roman minds.

But (according to Luke) the kingdom of Christ preached was not only universal but peaceable, and the 'son of David' had proved to be after all the prince of peace. It was promised that the day which dawned with Jesus would 'guide our feet into the way of peace' — so ran the opening pages of *Luke* — while angels who announced Christ's birth echoed the promise with 'Glory to God in the highest, and on earth peace . . .'

And so it proved. Not even biblical precedent could stir Christ into calling down fire to punish insulting Samaritans (9:51–56), and when he sent out the emissaries of his kingdom their first word at every house they entered was to be 'Peace!' (10:5, 'Shalom!', the familiar Jewish greeting, but Luke would read more into the unfamiliar gesture). In private relationships, Christ's counsel was for conciliation 'on the way', before implacable antagonism made a bad situation worse (12:58–59). Such creative readiness for conciliation and healing is also expressed as a command: 'If your brother sins

. . . against you seven times in the day, and turns to you seven times and says "I repent", you must forgive him' (17:3–4).

The point is thrust still further home in the command to 'Love your enemies, do good to those who hate you, bless those who curse you, pray for those who abuse you. To him who strikes you on the cheek' (the insufferable insult) 'offer the other also; and from him who takes away your cloak' (the intolerable injustice) 'do not withhold your coat as well . . . And as you wish that men *would do* to you, do so to them' (6:27–31).

As Jesus came to the capital to challenge decision about himself, he rode unarmed upon a colt, attended by peasant pilgrims amid hymns of praise, 'Blessed be the king who comes in the name of the Lord! Peace in heaven and glory in the highest!' And as he drew near and saw the city he wept over it, 'Would that even today you knew the things that make for peace! But now they are hid from your eyes'. This was no guerrilla leader!

In one brief but revealing paragraph Luke shows that this ideal of a kingdom of peace was not talk only, but the application of a deep principle of behaviour; indeed, it implied a radical change of personality. A long-smouldering dispute among the disciples of the kingdom shadowed the last weeks, or months, of Christ's ministry. The cause was personal rivalry — which of them was to be regarded as the greatest, and Luke evidently felt it to be serious, for he refers to it three times.

> At Caesarea Philippi, according to Matthew, Jesus had singled out Peter for special praise, speaking of 'rock' and 'keys'. Luke does not record this promise, but he does say that when, eight days later, Jesus had chosen only Peter, James and John to witness his transfiguration, 'an argument arose' among the Twelve as to which of them was the greatest. Luke notes that Jesus perceived their thoughts, and read them the lesson of childlike humility, the *least* being the greatest (Mark adds that he must be last of all and *servant* of all). The contention, however, did not end there. We know (Mark 10:35–45, Matthew 20:20–28) that James and John attempted to secure places at Christ's right and left in the kingdom, and this made the rest 'indignant'. On this occasion too Jesus had spoken plainly of the greatness which seeks to 'lord it' over others and exercise authority, adding 'it shall not be so among you; whoever would be great among you must be your servant . . . slave of all. For the Son of man also came not to be served but to serve', and, as the culmination of that service, 'to give his life as a ransom for many'. Luke further records that Jesus took advantage of an invitation to dine, to speak of the wisdom of taking lower places until asked to 'go up higher', because 'every one who exalts himself shall be

humbled, and he who humbles himself shall be exalted.' (Luke calls this a *parable*, hinting deeper truth.)

In spite of these repeated and forthright words, the dispute broke out yet again, possibly occasioned by the special trust reposed in James and John, in sending them forward to prepare the secret rendezvous for the Passover supper. At this point Luke records the saying about the world's 'great' ones and 'benefactors' loving to exercise dominion over others. 'But not so with you; rather let the greatest among you become as the youngest, and the leader as one who serves . . . I am among you as one who serves.'

This long-running contention within the disciple-band concerned, of course, their dearest hopes (Matthew 19:27), and struck to the root of human nature — its self-seeking, its ambition, its eagerness to put others down, its will to dominate with power and demonstrate authority. *Such is the ultimate cause of all strife, in all ages* (compare James 4:1–3). The only possible antidote to such striving *against* each other is to strive *for* each other, total dedication to the service of others. Only when in place of inter-personal rivalry and contention is substituted inter-personal appreciation, concern, and service, is peace conceivable, let alone attainable. But this involves a radical re-orientation of personality — another definition of repentance — in which self is redirected to outgoing good will in place of dominating self-love (compare 2 Corinthians 5:15).

The motive for such a peace-creating change of attitude lies not in Christ's teaching alone, though that is powerful. The tyrants who, on their coins, called themselves 'Benefactors', and the kings like Herod whose 'lordship' was widely hated, provided reason enough why 'it shall not be so' in the kingdom of God. To that reasoning, however, Jesus added his own example, which they had witnessed and marvelled at many times: 'I am among you as one who serves'. Loyalty to him demanded a like self-effacing service.

But even more, they themselves were deeply indebted to his service, and would be more so, when that service was crowned by his giving his life a ransom for theirs. This was the final argument. The king who saved them, at infinite cost, called for like service of men, in his name, in all circumstances. That is the sure, and the only, foundation of peace among men of good will.

At the moment of arrest, when under the tension of crisis true motives tend to be exposed, Jesus faced the most dangerous moment of his whole mission. For 'those who were about him', seeing what would follow, said, 'Lord, shall we strike with the sword?' and instantly upon the suggestion one of them struck the slave of the high priest, cutting off his ear. For a second, the whole nature of Christ's cause, the whole future of the Christian movement, stood poised in peril. This one act could have undone the years of ministry, of reinterpreting the messiahship and the kingdom, and justified the authorities in their suspicion and bitter opposition. 'But Jesus said . . . ' (How clearly and forcefully Luke clarifies the position for Theophilus!) 'But Jesus said, "No more of this!" And he touched the slave's ear and healed him.' Then he turned to the priests, captains, and elders, and blamed them for using violence. His immediate response to his followers' show of force was obviously successful, for the incident was not mentioned at his trial.

When at last Jesus stood face to face with the highest 'Excellency' in the province, the Governor Pilate, accused of 'perverting the nation, forbidding to give tribute to Caesar, and saying that he himself is Christ, a king', it was to hear Rome's mouthpiece declare repeatedly 'I find no crime in this man . . . I do not find this man guilty of any of your charges against him'. For Luke's readers, there could be no stronger testimony to the peaceable nature of the kingdom of God.

Two comments of Jesus might throw a shade of doubt upon this consistent picture of a king of peaceable intention and a kingdom without violence. As the modern world knows only too well, the will to peace does not ensure peace, and at what was evidently a moment of tension, Jesus vividly describes the unwelcome effect of his coming and ministry among those who refused him. He came to cast fire on the earth, and how he wished it were already kindled; he faced a baptism of suffering, and how he was under pressure until it was accomplished! 'Do you think,' he asked sadly, 'that I have come to give peace on earth?' — to which the answer of his whole teaching and ministry would be 'Yes!' But it was not so working out. His tension, suffering, and danger, were being shared by others. Loyalty to him was unfortunately breaking up families. 'No, I tell you, but rather division; for henceforth in one house there will be five divided . . . father against son . . . mother . . . daughter . . . daughter-in-law . . .' It was not his purpose, yet it would happen. Disciples were called to renounce every conflict caused by ambition, the will-to-power, or self-aggrandisement, only to find themselves involved in deeper conflict with all that hinders God's kingdom. Thus they must undergo his own baptism of pain, actually sharing in the cross which alone could bring peace and reconciliation to mankind.

And at the end, in the last moments alone with his men, Jesus strove to prepare them for the difficult, perilous future ahead for them. Once they could go out without purse or food, bag or sandals, relying on the good will of many to support earnest men speaking truth. Now it would be very different. Purse and bag should be taken, and — in his usual picturesque, memorable way he added — 'let him who has no sword sell his mantle and buy one'. So dangerous will their life be henceforth. As so often, uncomprehending disciples took his words literally. 'Look, Lord, here are two swords.' And he said to them with great sadness, 'That's enough!' (RSV; NEB 'Enough! Enough!'). If they do not understand now, only reflection on his teaching, and experience, will teach them.

Luke's transmutation of the kingdom hope to one of present spiritual experience of life under God's rule, shared by all races, wholly alien to the power drives, ambitions and violence of the kingdoms of this world, was radical and far-reaching. It could unite the world; within it, peace not conquest was the sign of victory, the proof of strength. Luke's readers could appreciate both the challenge and the appeal of that programme and vision. In its light, Christianity was a gospel for mankind, which might yet save the Roman empire from disaster.

But what of the evil that frustrates all human aspiration?

CHAPTER 8
The Evil That Men Do

Christian emphasis upon love, compassion, and peace, descends easily to useless sentimentality unless the presence of evil, within society and in individuals, is frankly and realistically faced. Luke knew that his audience of responsible leaders of Roman society were more keenly aware than most of the problems posed by criminals, rebels, 'social misfits', and antisocial egotists. Roman law and Statecraft were probably the best in history; but laws and punishments had not prevented a steady deterioration of society in the first century. Already there were early signs of the complete decay that was ultimately to weaken the empire before her external enemies.

Writing to Rome itself, Paul draws a grim picture of wickedness, suppression of truth, lust, carnality, unnatural perversions, evil covetousness, envy, murder, strife, deceit, pride, family disintegration, want of integrity, and much else (Romans 1:18–32, compare 2 Thessalonians 2:6–8). Paul had travelled much of the Roman world, and his foreboding is abundantly confirmed by secular observers, historians, and satirists, who describe the general corruption, sensuality, and wasteful luxury, of the later empire. The strictures and warnings of pagan moralists like Seneca and Epictetus, underline these features of contemporary society, while slavery, infanticide, religious prostitution, suicide, bloodthirsty cruelties in the arenas, hardly raised protest. Moral corruption, 'prevailing, penetrating, and subtly pervasive' gave to officials of Theophilus' class serious cause for social concern. Some reaction had been provoked. A kind of religious awakening, in the Mystery Religions and similar cults, in various reform societies supporting itinerant preachers and 'revivalists' (such as Paul was taken to be, at Athens) began to create an awareness of social peril in which the earnest idealism of Christianity could find a hearing. But their influence was limited.

Christ's Realism

Luke therefore would have his Roman readers see clearly how Jesus confronted moral evil, although the social and domestic standard within Jewry was in most respects higher than in the Graeco-Roman world. Together, the Gospels provide an astonishing list of over thirty evil-minded rascals whom Jesus acutely observed and relentlessly described. Of these, Luke sets before us:

The professional prostitute, whose sins were many (ch 7)
The heartless priest, unconscious of social duty (10)
The indifferent Levite, ignoring the needy (10)
The churlish neighbour, impatient of a simple request (11)
The hypocritical Pharisees, hiding the truth (12)
The blasphemer against light, beyond forgiveness (12)
The money-making farmer, with no thought above his barns (12)
The callous legalists, valuing regulations above suffering (13)
The crafty king, ruling by vulpine cunning (13)
The trivial-minded, offering childish excuses (14)
The ungrateful youth, rebelling against restraint (15)
The dishonest steward, embezzling his master's capital (16)
The unfeeling glutton, ignoring the beggar at his door (16)
The corrupter of children, better never born (17)
The slave-driving boss, demanding his supper at once (17)
The unjust judge, needing to be plagued into doing his duty (18)
The self-righteous Pharisee, parading his piety (18)
The lazy servant, hoarding money entrusted for use (19)
The flattery-loving scribe, delighting in obsequious tributes (20)
The ruthless moneylender, mortgaging a widow's home (20)
The faithless disciples, carousing in their Lord's absence (21)
The treacherous disciple, who betrays the Master (22)
The tyrant rulers, called benefactors because overbearing (22)
The shallow friend, boasting yet denying (22).

To these character-sketches should be added more general observations of Jesus, as of lawyers who made religion burdensome for ordinary people, or who by hugging knowledge to themselves in academic or technical language deprived others of the truth; of Pharisees who 'were lovers of money', external in their judgements, lacking a true sense of priorities (11:42); the prodigal's elder brother, without affection or forgiveness; and ruthless social climbers (14:7). Luke leaves us in no doubt that Jesus saw clearly the evil attitudes and poses that afflict society.

It is important, however, to understand what Jesus considered to be evil, for in several ways he differed sharply from the moral judgements of his contemporaries. He did not rank breaches of the sabbath rules at all important, if others' pain or helplessness could be cured; nor (as Theophilus will be glad to note) did Jesus hold himself aloof from Jewish tax collectors serving Rome at the cost of their countrymen's respect. Jesus thought less than did the pious around him of external ritual cleanness (11:37–41), of prescribed and habitual fasting, as evidence of righteousness. Selfishness and self-righteousness were to his mind worse evils than the sins of the flesh, and often more cruel. Luke tends to emphasize such differences between Jesus and the Jewish leaders, perhaps to explain the prevalent Jewish antipathy to Christianity in the Roman world.

On the other hand, Luke shows Jesus expressing moral disapproval, in varying degrees, of adultery, harlotry, loose living (16:18, 15:13, 30); of Herod's imprisonment of John for rebuking adultery; of all hypocrisy, ostentation, and pride; of vindictiveness (9:55), indecision (9:57–62), fruitless living (13:6–9), covetousness (12:15), egotistic selfishness (12:17–21 — eleven first-personal pronouns!). Jesus condemns ingratitude, attempting God's work in ungodly ways (4:1–12), flattery (11:27), evil intention cloaked with piety (6:8–9), and the cowardice that could make disciples ashamed of his name (9:26). And Jesus sharply rebuked 'faithless and perverse' disciples (9:41, compare Matthew 17:17 where there is no crowd), blasphemy (12:10), inconsistency (13:14–15, 14:5), drunkenness and gluttony (21:34), betrayal (22:47–48), the cloak of darkness and violence (22:52–53), withholding God's due (20:11, 25), and dishonest monopoly profiteering from others' worship (19:46).

It is hard to see where the notion that Jesus saw only good in all people could have arisen; according to Luke Jesus considered men themselves as evil (11:13), sometimes possessed by evil (11:26), and making up 'an evil generation' (11:29). No one has ground for judging his brother (6:41–42). But often the terms used are general, even vague. 'Sin, sinful' usually includes any 'missing of the ideal, of life's real aim'; 'evil' usually connotes 'bad, worthless, wicked'; 'workers of iniquity' (13:27) indicates especially behaviour that is not 'right', any injustice; and 'offenders' (13:4) strictly means those who owe a duty and do not pay it. Roman readers could apply such expressions in the widest way, according to what they felt to be reprehensible in society.

Nevertheless, according to Luke, people are not in Jesus' eyes entirely bad, or 'totally depraved'. 'Even sinners love those who love them . . . do good to those who do good to them . . . lend to sinners' (6:32–34). Some had responded to John's preaching, when religious leaders had not (7:29). The word of God was sometimes held fast 'in an honest and good heart' (8:15); even more significantly, Christ could appeal to his hearers to 'judge for yourselves what is right' (12:57).

Yet evil does exist. Jesus does not theorize about its origin, but simply traces it to the individual's inward life and nature. 'No good tree bears bad fruit, nor again does a bad tree bear good fruit . . . the good man out of the good treasure of his heart produces good . . . the evil man . . . evil; for out of the abundance of the heart his mouth speaks' (6:43–45; 'out of the overflowing' NEB). That is why external ritual cleanliness could conceal 'inside . . . extortion and wickedness', and why it was imperative to cleanse the inside, when the outer life would be clean also (11:38–41; 'give alms' probably mistranslates an Aramaic word, see Matthew 23:25–26). An external show of piety can justify in man's eyes, but God knows the heart (16:15).

From one point of view, this inward view of evil as something belonging to personality itself makes evil more serious. Jesus never excuses, condones, or minimizes human wrongdoing. The consequences of sin are spelled out relentlessly. Beside the lonely wretchedness, pigs' food, and hunger of rebellion (15:14–17), God has power to cast evil-doers into Ge Hinnom (12:5; the valley outside Jerusalem where rubbish burned and offal rotted — a picture of ultimate decay, degradation, and destruction). To place oneself beyond the illumination of the Spirit on what is good and what evil, is to be already beyond forgiveness (12:10, interpreted by Matthew 12:24–32). 'Severe beating' or 'light beating', according to a man's privileges and opportunities, await the disobedient (12:47–48). Eventually, doors will shut against the careless, the banquet be withheld (13:25, 14:24); those who corrupt others had better not live; accounts must be rendered and wrongs righted (17:11, 16:2, 19–31). To Herod, who had killed John, Jesus had nothing to say (23:9). Sinners will not be allowed to shrug off responsibility, saying, 'Such I was, I could not help it'.

Because, from another point of view, the fact that evil originates within the personality is hopeful; personalities can be changed. Sin is, in this respect, a sickness calling for a physician (5:31). Peter's sinfulness was no insuperable barrier to his being called to discipleship — with Christ's help (5:1–11). And the reputation of Levi the tax collector and his friends offered no reason why Jesus should not associate with them (5:27–32). The prime need was for repentance, a total rethinking of one's attitudes, from which total change of lifestyle would follow. Repentance also brought about a totally new relation to God; the penitent is always, and immediately, 'justified' in God's sight (7:29, 18:14).

The Power of Repentance

Hence, in Luke's Gospel, recalling Jesus' own emphasis, repentance is of first importance. Jesus had come expressly to call sinners to repentance (5:32). His warning is, 'repent or perish' (13:1–5). John had preached with the same note: be baptised in repentance or be baptised in fire (3:16–17)! It is never too late to repent, while life lasts, as the dying thief discovered, but to refuse repentance, in spite of Christ's word and work, as Chorazin, Bethsaida, Capernaum had done, was to prove oneself worse than pagan Tyre, Sidon and ancient Nineveh. In the end impenitence would involve a fate worse than theirs (10:13–15, 11:32). Implacable obduracy would find no cure, even in the next world, as the rich man learned in Hades (16:29–31). Though God is very patient, fruitless trees must eventually be cut down (13:6–9).

The crucial question, for the sinner, for Theophilus and his colleagues, for society, as for ourselves, was how in face of evil in the heart such repentance was to be evoked. Luke's answer is: by the presence of Christ. He was named Jesus (the Greek form of Joshua, 'God is salvation', or as a contemporary of Jesus interpreted it, 'Salvation is of the Lord'). Luke does not explain the name, presumably because it was one subject on which Theophilus would have been correctly informed; but Luke confirms the promise contained in the name, by showing that John will go before the Lord to give 'knowledge of salvation' in the forgiveness of sins (1:76–77), and by recording the words of the angels, 'a Saviour, who is Christ, the Lord'. The promise of 'redemption' in Zechariah's song has more to do with 'deliverance from . . . our enemies' than with salvation from sin; but in the thought of Anna, the prophetess 'looking for the redemption of Jerusalem', something more religious than political was probably intended (2:38, compare 24:21).

Luke repeatedly shows the presence of Jesus kindling repentance: in Peter (5:8), in Levi and his friends (5:27–32), in a sinful woman (7:38), in Zaccheus (19:8), and in the dying thief (23:42). The whole climax, purpose, and summary of Christ's earthly ministry is so expressed by Luke himself, 'that repentance and forgiveness of sins should be preached in his name' (24:45). This is what earned for Jesus the reproach, which Luke plainly takes to be a compliment, 'Friend of tax collectors and sinners' (7:34), and the constant criticism that he should associate with such people (5:30, 15:2). Sometimes his presence is forcibly expressed in the authoritative announcement of forgiveness, as to the paralysed man, something in whose manner, or inherited opinions about sickness and sin, made such a declaration appropriate in his case (5:20, 24, compare 7:48–49). Such announcement of forgiveness immediately kindled hope, and change.

Repentance, however (still according to Luke's record of Christ's teaching), was not merely a change of attitude, or a feeling of regret. The Baptist had spelled out the radical change of behaviour which repentance involved for ordinary people, for tax collectors, and for soldiers of the occupying force (3:10–14), and Jesus was no less forthright. True repentance meant denying the self that had hitherto been the centre and focus of life, taking up the cross daily, following Christ, willingness to lose life for his sake, and to forfeit the world, and even one's family if need be, for salvation's sake (9:23–25, 14:26; the word salvation occurs thirteen times in *Luke-Acts*, not at all in Matthew, Mark). Any attempt to preserve the old life would forfeit the new (17:33). Repentance required also resolution, to forego comfort, leave lesser responsibilities to others, and give immediate and unregretting dedication — nothing less was 'fit for the kingdom of God' (9:57–62).

Repeatedly, Jesus called for more than a change of mood, which might be short-lived. He required repentant action — 'Go . . . Do . . . Obey . . . and you will live' (10:28, 37, to a lawyer seeking eternal life); 'Strive to enter . . .' (13:24, to one asking how many would be saved); 'You know the commandments . . .' (18:20, to another who asked 'What shall I do to inherit eternal life?' and who on refusing Christ's terms was allowed to go away). Repentance could not be mere negative self-reform: the evil exorcised must be replaced by good (11:24–26). The 'sifting as wheat' that alone could build new character was not to be evaded, even by Christ's prayers (22:31–32). Such action, striving, dedication to good, in no way earned salvation, but it was necessary to demonstrate the reality of repentance, the genuine desire to change, and in the truly penitent it would be freely forthcoming, with gladness.

Nor (once again) did repentance mean instant and complete salvation. 'Temptations to sin are sure to come' (17:1); repeated, daily prayer is necessary, both for renewed forgiveness (11:4, the Lord's prayer), and for protection (also 11:4, and in Gethsemane, 22:40, 46). Yet, though such continued striving, prayer, and watchfulness are needed, repentance does bring immediate joy, in heaven and on earth (15: 6–7, 9–10, 24, 32).

A leader of Roman society, deeply concerned about the moral problems of his time, could hardly miss the relevance of these insights scattered through Luke's Gospel, or their clear implication, that Christianity was no mere Mystery cult or emotional indulgence, but an earnest religious attempt to deal with the real problems of sinful men. But lest the significance of this gospel against evil should be lost on any reader, Luke provides several cameos of the saving process at work, which together make a memorable impact.

Salvation Illustrated

One cameo shows the call of Peter to apostleship (5:1–11). Though we have to read between the lines to see the implication, two things are clear. Christ's success at fishing, where the experts trying all night had failed, reduced Peter to the confession of his sinfulness; and the call to follow, with the promise that eventually he would 'catch men' instead of fish, Christ making him successful where hitherto he had failed, completely won Peter's allegiance. Just what Peter's 'sinfulness' consisted in, we can only guess, though we find later that Peter is impulsive, emotional, unreliable, and (just once) hard-swearing. John tells us that Jesus had met Peter (perhaps previously) and given him the new name which means 'rock' (John 1:42). We may surmise that meanwhile Peter had striven to live up to that new name, and failed, discovering his own sinfulness. The miraculous catch of fish, and the call to discipleship, come as a strong promise that with Christ in command he shall yet succeed. That is, at any rate, an impressive illustration of Christ at work in sinful lives.

The second cameo shows us the 'sinful woman' in the house of Simon the Pharisee (7:36–50), a truly magnificent story, not least as demonstrating the strong indignation of Jesus. The woman's 'penitence' is silent, but dramatic, her devoted actions and her tears saying all. The cold logic of the Pharisee sets off both her emotion and Christ's in perfect contrast. Yet Jesus' words are incisive. The story of the two debtors, by which Christ elicited from Simon himself the gospel-principle — that they will love most who most have been forgiven — states the rationale of Christianity's method with evil, beyond all argument. Jesus does not deny that her sins 'are many', but his assurance of forgiveness, and the kind dismissal, 'Your faith has saved you, go into peace' set a divine seal on Christian moral redemption.

The third cameo is the superb trilogy of parables in chapter 15, spoken in answer to the criticism, 'This man receives sinners and eats with them'. Between them the parables illustrate three ways of becoming 'lost' — little by little, by foolish 'nibbling'; by mere carelessness; by wilful and ungrateful rebellion. And three ways of being found — by the sacrificial searching of one to whom the sheep was valuable (hired shepherds had to pay for any losses); by the eager searching of one to whom the coin (or bridal decoration? — the word represents an antique coin) was a sore loss; by the long hard trudge homewards to a welcoming father, retracing the wrong done, step by weary step. Neither sheep nor coin nor son is recovered by its or his own effort alone, and there is joy in heaven and earth over each restoration.

Because of the nature of the stories, repentance is illustrated only in the case of the prodigal; and only in his experience is there opposition, that of the Pharisees whose criticism evoked the parables. The prodigal's elder brother sees no justice in this joyous welcome to the young rascal. And there is none. In 'the salvation of evil men, it is not justice but grace which operates. Eloquently, Jesus makes no comment on the elder brother, except (in effect), 'Just look at him! Listen to him!'

The fourth cameo of Christian salvation at work is the story of Zaccheus (19:1–10), probably of even more interest to Theophilus and his friends. For Zaccheus was apparently a 'commissioner' of taxes for an area ('superintendent of taxes' NEB), and Roman Governors and magistrates must often have had to deal with fraudulent tax officials, recruited from occupied peoples into the service of Rome. Perhaps that is why only Luke tells of this voluntary transformation to total honesty, and even more, to great generosity, by an agent operating in one of the most turbulent and resentful provinces of the empire.

The initiative in this instance lay wholly with Jesus, though enough interest is shown by Zaccheus to place him in the way of penitence. 'Conversion' here is moral and financial rather than mystical; and Christ's final verdict on the man, that 'he also is a son of Abraham' and not merely 'a sinner' (as onlookers said), reveals one aspect of Christian strategy: treat a man as the best he has it in him to be, and he will often rise to attain it. The final comment on this incident crystallizes the whole theme in twelve words; 'the Son of man came to seek and to save the lost'.

Jesus and Salvation

It has been said that in these stories of individual salvation there is no necessary place for either Jesus himself or for his death. 'The prodigal needed no saviour.' Yet, in Luke, in nearly every instance, Christ is central, the initiator, calling to discipleship, pronouncing forgiveness, defending against criticism, offering friendship, declaring the divine purpose to save, adding the strong assurance of acceptance, dignity, and peace. Even the story of the prodigal is told only to explain and justify Christ's attitude towards sinners; and the effect of the story – Christ's story, with his authority behind it — has been to assure others of a welcome to the loving Father's home if they will return.

Without Christ, in *Luke*, there would have been no stories of changed lives, and no gospel of salvation. The reason for the 'necessity' of Christ's death is perhaps less clear. Luke does not, like Matthew, allow the sayings of Jesus at the end to illuminate the meaning of his death, especially the covenant and sacrificial terms used at the last supper. Nor does he, like Mark, preserve the significant 'ransom' saying (Mark 10:45), which recalls Isaiah 53 and sets Christ's death in the context of service to others. Nor yet does Luke, as did John, link Christ's death directly to the Passover lambs and the suffering Servant of Isaiah's prophecies. Probably because to Theophilus, the Gentile, this language would not be familiar, perhaps hardly intelligible.

It has been suggested that in *Luke* Jesus leads the new Israel through a new exodus experience from slavery to freedom, and that this explains why, on the mountain of transfiguration, Moses and Elijah are said to have spoken with Jesus of the 'exodus' Jesus would accomplish at Jerusalem (9:31). But it is hard to find this idea anywhere in *Luke*; the word 'exodus' means simply 'death' in 2 Peter 1:15, and in six other places in early Christian literature, and so probably meant simply 'death' to Luke's readers. Nor does Jesus speak of the Passover feast, or story, being 'fulfilled' in his death, but in the kingdom of God (22:16). What, then, did Luke wish Theophilus to understand concerning Christ's death?

First, it is clear that Christ's death was necessary to the fulfilment of his mission. As early as 9:51 Luke speaks of the days drawing near 'for him to be received up', using a rare word meaning 'to be taken up', 'ascension', or (as elsewhere) simply a euphemism for 'death'. That a plan or programme was to be worked through, which included Jesus' death, seems implied, and becomes unmistakable in sayings like 'O foolish men, and slow of heart to believe all that the prophets have spoken! Was it not necessary that the Christ should suffer these things and enter into his glory?' Luke adds, 'And beginning with Moses and all the prophets, he interpreted to them in all the scriptures the things concerning himself.' Again, 'These are my words which I spoke to you while I was still with you, that everything written about me in the law of Moses and the prophets and the psalms must be fulfilled . . . Thus it is written, that the Christ should suffer and on the third day rise from the dead' (24:26–27, 44, 46). So Jesus explained what was troubling his hearers, his passion, rejection, and death, as things that should have been obvious. Such opening of 'their minds to understand the scriptures' was only possible after the event, but Jesus had sought repeatedly to prepare the disciples for this prophesied climax to his ministry (9:22, 17:25, 22:37), as the resurrection-angel reminded them (24:7).

This necessity of dying, as of something divinely planned and often foretold, robs Christ's death of any air of tragedy, anticlimax, or defeat. Nor was Jesus in any sense a helpless victim of 'fate', of man's evildoing, or of divine omnipotence. 'The Son of man goes as it has been determined' (22:22) combines divine purpose with willing obedience. And because Jesus has died and risen again, the plan of his life has been fulfilled, and henceforth 'repentance and forgiveness of sins should be preached in his name to all nations' as was intended (24:47).

Even so, the inner necessity of this programme — just *why* Jesus' death was prophesied and fulfilled in order that repentance and forgiveness might be offered to men — Luke does not makes clear. Two details of the story, which only Luke records, probably reveal his mind. Unfortunately one is textually doubtful; it is the sublime prayer ascribed to Jesus upon the cross, 'Father, forgive them; for they know not what they do' (23:34; so RSV 1946, 1971, with footnote mentioning omission by some authorities; NEB 1970, with similar footnote; United Bible Societies Greek Testament 3rd edition, retains within brackets signifying doubt, the committee feeling that the prayer is genuine, but not in the earliest copies of Luke). If the prayer is in fact a genuine part of Luke's Gospel, it fittingly summarizes the intention of Jesus' death for all sinners, and not only for those concerned in the crucifixion.

There is no such doubt about the other detail, an interpretative comment by Jesus upon his death, and one wholly consonant with the story Luke has told, of a friend of sinners intent upon siding with, coming alongside, and saving 'the lost'. In 22:37 Jesus says, 'I tell you that this scripture must be fulfilled in me, "And he was reckoned with transgressors"; for what is written about me has its fulfilment.' Like so many other phrases applied in the New Testament to the death of Jesus, the words are taken from Isaiah 53, and they wonderfully recall Christ's constant identification with sinful men and women — with Peter and the paralysed man, with Levi and the sinful woman, with the lost lamb and the prodigal, with Zaccheus and the dying thief ('*with me* in Paradise'). It was this self-identification with the ostracized and condemned that evoked the bitterest criticism of Jesus, in Luke's Gospel; through it, he shared the ostracism and condemnation. So he died as he had ministered, between two transgressors, reckoned with them and rejected with them, and in consequence saving the penitent one of them. That is at least a major part of Luke's explanation of the cross.

All in all, Luke's message concerning evil and personal salvation is a marvellously hopeful gospel for individuals. But Luke saw, in the Christian movement he had met, much more than this. He saw a motive and a power making for wider moral reform, for social rehabilitation of the wrongdoers and misfits that threatened the general welfare. And he would have Theophilus know it. It is a serious question whether before long this simple gospel of the forgiveness of sins and renewal of the sinner may not once again move to the centre of attention, in the revulsion and aftermath that must follow a 'permissive', and socially destructive, era.

CHAPTER 9

Christian Humanism

The wide interest which Luke shows in the alien and outsider, in the sinful and despised, and in problems of peace among rival and antagonistic groups, does not stop there. At least three further areas of social concern are explored in his Gospel as he studies the ministry of Jesus. Taken together, these emphases constitute a characteristic, almost a unique, interpretation of the gospel of Christ.

Ministry to the Sick

We might expect that as a physician Luke would show keen interest in Christ's dealings with the sick and those afflicted with various ills, deficiencies, and handicaps. In that ancient world the sick were everywhere, for life was harsh, and medicine relatively primitive. The sick are everywhere in the Gospels, too, but Luke, seeing with a doctor's eye and describing with a doctor's accuracy, values Christ's ministry among them as perhaps only a doctor would.

When John sent to Jesus asking, 'Are you he who is to come?', Luke comments that in that hour Jesus cured many of diseases and plagues and evil spirits, and on many that were blind he bestowed sight. And Jesus answered, 'Go, tell John what you have seen and heard, the blind receive their sight, the lame walk, lepers are cleansed, the deaf hear, the dead are raised, and the poor have good news preached to them. And blessed is he who takes no offence at me.' For Luke, as for Jesus, that was answer enough. Not only were the words of Isaiah (29:18–19) being wonderfully fulfilled, but the healing and consolation of the sick, in body and in mind, was evidence sufficient that the kingdom of God had come.

Where motives and reactions are mentioned at all, Mark sets the healing miracles of Jesus six times in a context of wonder, six times in an atmosphere of controversy, and mentions pity *once*. Matthew sets them thirteen times amid wonder, three times in controversy, and *once* in relation to pity. Luke mentions wonder four times, controversy five times, and either mentions compassion, or expresses it in the telling, *seven times*. The comparison — such as it is — has a certain significance. Jews usually ascribed sickness and affliction to individual sin, which seriously inhibited compassion. Sometimes they explained suffering by demon possession, but with the hint that the patient's behaviour let the demon in. Pagans ascribed most sickness to witchcraft, or to fate; neither explanation left room for pity or for hope.

Luke had noticed that Christians, following Jesus, denied that sickness was always direct punishment for sin. They accepted the prevalent ideas about demons, but insisted that Jesus had conquered them, so that the sufferer was not helpless. And they cared less about explaining suffering than about curing it. Luke noticed too that Jesus never recoiled from the spectacle of disease, infirmity, or madness, but touched the leper, allowed the 'unclean' to touch him without rebuke, held conversation with the deranged, spoke gently to those who in their distress challenged him (4:34), and sprang to the defence of the maimed or diseased who obtruded themselves into synagogues or rich men's houses (13:10–14:2).

Luke retells twelve healing miracles told by other evangelists, and adds five of his own recovering, together with five summaries recording innumerable and varied cures, of which no details survive (4:40–41, 5:15, 6:17–19, 7:22–23, 9:1, 6, 11). He obviously makes no attempt at a complete record; indeed, he strongly suggests that such would be impossible; but of the importance he attached to this healing ministry there can be no doubt.

In the healing stories shared with the other Gospels, Luke makes numerous small changes. For example, he adds that the servant of the centurion was 'dear' to him; also that both Jairus' daughter and the epileptic boy were 'only' children. Jesus 'rebuked' the 'high fever' affecting Peter's mother-in-law, while the man 'full of leprosy' fell on his face before Jesus. When the paralytic was brought to Jesus, Luke mentions that 'the power of the Lord was with Jesus to heal'. Being less familiar with Palestine, Luke says the man was let down through the 'tiles' (Mark says they 'dug through' the (wattle) roof). Luke omits the natural Aramaic which Jesus spoke to Jairus' daughter ('Talitha, cumi'), substituting the formal Greek 'Child, arise!' The hand Jesus restored was the right hand (implying that the man could now work again; tradition says he was a stone mason). Luke says the demon 'shattered' the epileptic boy, and he omits the colloquy with the disciples which followed. Oddly, Luke does not give the name of the blind man Jesus healed, 'Bartimaeus', nor mention the vivid detail that he threw away his mantle to get to Jesus more quickly. Plainly, if the information Luke gives is shared by others, Luke gives it always in his own way, with freshness and thought.

If we need any explanation of the five healings Luke adds from his own researches, it is not hard to find. In the raising of the dead outside Nain, the deep sorrow of a widow who has lost her only son and support, which moved Christ's compassion, and the powerful effect on the countryside, are sufficient reasons for recording the story. But it also prepares for the answer sent to John, which immediately follows; no other raising of the dead had yet occurred. The releasing of the woman bowed and 'bound' illustrates one of Luke's great themes, Christ's ministry to women.

The presence in a Pharisee's house of a man suffering from dropsy (14:1–4) posed in its sharpest form the issue between Jesus' instant compassion and the rigid, logical legalism of the stricter Jews. Jesus takes the initiative, with his question about the legality of healing on the sabbath. The lawyers' silence was due to unresolved arguments among various authorities, and it forfeited the right to criticize afterwards. Jesus' reminder of their ready rescue of property (or of a son) on the sabbath, was unanswerable. The healing of the ten lepers involved Luke's interest in Christ's comments upon aliens, while the healing of the slave's right ear was imperative, to silence any accusation of armed resistance to arrest. In neither of these three stories is any more personal motive mentioned.

Luke seems to have felt that endless stories of this kind could be told, and he has included those which, for varying reasons, had special interest or implications. The over-riding impression left by Luke's treatment of Christ's healings is that he considered them a most significant part of Christ's ministry, a clear manifestation of the gracious nature of God's kingdom, and evidence sufficient that a new power was at work in the world, and available to men through Christ. At the same time, nothing remotely resembling a 'healing campaign', offering 'signs and wonders' to the gaping multitudes, is recorded. Christ's miracle ministry was for healing and pity only.

Thus, Jesus did not allow the incessant call for healing to distract him from the preaching of the kingdom. Sometimes he withdrew to other places (4:42–43), or to the wilderness (5:16), or checked enthusiasm over wonders with warning of his approaching death (9:43–45). The same restraint concerning miracles is evident in his forthright reminder that power over the spirits is not the true basis of Christian joy, but the far greater privilege of having one's name written in heaven (10:20). Nor did Jesus at any point modify his original resolve that the kingdom could not be built upon signs and wonders (4:3–4, 9–12). A generation which demanded 'signs' of God's truth and power was 'evil' — incapable of the moral judgement which would discern God wherever he spoke and acted. The only 'sign' vouchsafed to such was 'the sign of Jonah', a prophet preaching truth. Those who could not perceive his authority, or John's, for themselves, would be given no clearer 'evidence'. Their need was for inward light (11:29–30, 32–36, 20:1–8). Indeed, exorcisms, 'miraculous' healings, signs and wonders of all kinds, were far too prevalent in that ancient world, within Jewry and around innumerable pagan temples, to provide 'evidence' of anything divine.

Nevertheless Luke evidently saw in the healing ministry of Jesus, and in the continuation of that ministry which he witnessed in the church, the possibility, and the promise, of widespread amelioration of suffering, a ground of renewal and of hope for an enormous section of society. And he would have Theophilus know it.

Ministry to Women

The place of women in Jewish society was ambiguous. Traditionally, Eve was blamed for all the evils in the world, and the Wisdom writings (*Proverbs* and *Sirach* especially) are full of warnings of women's allurements to sin. No woman was appointed priest, or allowed to enter the temple's holy place, while in the synagogues women were segregated from men, although very early 'women ministered at the door of the tent of meeting', whether in menial ways or musically is not known (Exodus 38:8, 1 Samuel 2:22). Pious Jews thanked God they had not been born women, and did not speak publicly even with their wives and daughters. Yet Sarah, Hannah, Deborah, the wise woman of Tekoa, Huldah the prophetess, Miriam, Esther, Judith, the mother of the Maccabeans, and the 'competent woman' of Proverbs 31:10–31 were greatly honoured.

Beyond Jewry, the persistent fear of something corrupting, and of witchcraft, was associated with womanhood, combined with stories of splendid heroines, and worshipful goddesses as patrons of the soil, hunting, wisdom, beauty, home-life, and as the Muses of art and science. Female oracles and priestesses abounded, and the Vestal virgins held Rome's fate in their hands. Nevertheless, slavery, religious and commercial prostitution, and usually want of education, oppressed most women. In some parts of Greece a 'woman's equality movement' aped male dress and public manners, and was beginning to find place for women in public affairs.

Luke is keenly aware of the great difference in women's position within Christianity, and his pages are crowded with women who find in Christ a new dignity and value. He names no less than twenty-six women participants in the story of the church, together with several groups. He twice notes Jesus' especial compassion for those 'daughters of Jerusalem' on whom the coming doom will bear so heavily (21:23, 23:28–29). He shows that women hailed Christ's birth, were last to leave the cross, and first announced Christ's resurrection.

Among nearly thirty very varied women mentioned by Luke are Elizabeth the pious Jewish matron, and Anna the aged prophetess; Susanna and Joanna of Herod's household, who ministered to Jesus' material needs; Mary from Magdala, in our terms probably insane and possibly immoral also; Mary and Martha, sisters beloved, whose home Jesus sometimes shared; and

Mary of Nazareth, of whom Luke tells us more than all other sources together, and whose character and story moved Luke to reverence and poetry.

Luke alone tells how a woman's tears over her dead son stirred Jesus' compassion to an act of resurrection power. A woman nagging a judge for justice gave him an illustration of persistent prayer, and another losing a coin from a headdress, an illustration of the value of the sinner to God. A woman making bread suggested to his mind the slow fermenting growth of the kingdom. The woman with haemorrhage was not allowed to disappear unnoticed in the crowd, but spoken to, and comforted. The young daughter of Jairus was most sensitively shielded from shock and notoriety. The widow who surreptitiously cast into the temple treasury a mere farthing earned his lasting commendation, and it was in defence of a woman, a sinner of the city, that Jesus blazed with indignation at seeing any woman treated with contempt.

> *Acts* continues the emphasis. 'The women' gather with the apostles in the house of Mary, mother of John Mark; at Pentecost, 'daughters and handmaidens' are assured the gift of the Spirit of prophecy; and four daughters of Philip are prophetesses, likewise; the Hebrew and the Hellenist widows serve the church in Jerusalem; Dorcas is 'full of good works and charity'; women shared in the severe persecution at Damascus; Lydia, whose heart God opened, and the Pythonness whom Paul cured share the opening of Europe to the gospel; Priscilla was the gifted teacher of Apollos; the maid Rhoda, Damaris the convert at Athens, 'leading women' in Thessalonica, and 'Greek women of high standing' at Berea, are all part of the Christian story as Luke tells it.

All these examples illustrate the incident, which Luke alone preserves, of the woman bound *by Satan*, bent over and unable to raise herself. Condemned for eighteen years to stumble through life with head down, she was released by Christ, lifted up, and set walking upright in the world, to look the rest of society in the face. So, Luke implies, Jesus has done for all women; and so, as we know, he has done for women in every land, and of every generation. 'She praised God': but the ruler of the synagogue objected, doubtless mindful of the prejudices which the story of Eve still nourished. He caught the sharp edge of Jesus' tongue in consequence. No wonder that 'all Christ's adversaries were put to shame', while 'all the people rejoiced at all the glorious things that were done by him'. They saw the significance of the miracle as clearly as Luke did.

The story of Martha and Mary entertaining Jesus in their home needs no solemn justification. But if it has a deeper meaning, it must lie in the contrast between the one woman 'busy about much serving', devoted to the kitchen and domestic cares, and the other woman who finds in the presence of Jesus a kindling of mind, and an opening of life to larger horizons, which Judaism denied her. Jesus' defence of Mary's eagerness to be taught is at any rate in direct contrast to the prevailing Jewish attitude, which held it a waste of effort, and a positive mischief, to teach women the Law. To underline that contrast may well have been Luke's intention in preserving the story.

Luke has seen in the Christian church a fairness, a tenderness, a dignity and opportunity, accorded to women that contrasted sharply with pagan ways and morals. In Christ a new era had dawned for women, offering liberation, equal value in God's sight, and wide social vocation — and Luke would have Theophilus know it.

Wealth and Poverty

Extremes of poverty and wealth constitute a major problem for society in every age, and theories about possession, the right to use, and communal ownership, were much canvassed in the ancient world as in our own. Though the right of private ownership was strongly defended in Jewish law, the imperative duty of almsgiving, and protection and provision for the widow, the fatherless, and the destitute, were rigorously demanded. The stricter Essenes frowned upon private property, sharing the use of tools, shelter, and daily provision, as at Qumran. On the other hand, Pharisees saw nothing wrong in riches, and earned a reputation as 'lovers of money' (16:14). Some saw prosperity as evidence of God's favour. Greek philosophers theorized about wealth and its distribution, and the problem of inequality faced Roman society in a perilous form in the existence of slavery. Free citizens were outnumbered five to one by slaves who, in Roman law, could own nothing. The social and economic dangers of this situation were rarely absent from official minds.

Luke again shows intense interest in the whole resulting problem, the thorniest of all questions of social responsibility. Mary's song at the Annunciation sounds almost revolutionary in affirming that God has scattered the proud, put down the mighty, filled the hungry with good things and sent the rich empty away. Luke alone, too, records the visit of the shepherds, a lower class of labourer, to the manger, and he betrays to us that the family of Jesus was among those accepted as poor (2:24, compare Leviticus 12:8). Luke shows that the counsel of the Baptist concentrated upon the ethics of property — share, be strictly honest, rob no one, be content. We are hardly surprised then to find the Nazareth sermon of Jesus declaring that his mission would be good news to the poor. That description is later repeated to John (7:22) as a mark of the kingdom of God.

Behind all that Jesus said about wealth and poverty lay his faith in the Father's care, as Luke makes clear (12:22–31). There is need, therefore, neither for avarice nor for anxiety; food, clothing are assured for God's children, as for birds, grass, lilies, men being of greater value in God's eyes than all other creatures. Let men only seek God's kingdom, and all necessary things shall be theirs.

Such confidence permits an attitude of detachment towards possessions and poverty. Jesus nowhere condemns riches, or praises, or recommends, poverty; both have spiritual dangers. He himself had rich friends, dined with them (7:36, 11:37, 14:1, 7), accepted their support (8:3). If (as is probable) 'partners' means shareholders in ownership of a vessel (5:10), then at least three disciples were not poor men; nor was Levi. At the end Jesus was 'with a rich man in his death' (23:50–53).

Renunciation of all possessions was not made a universal condition for entering the kingdom, though it was required of one 'very rich' man who desired eternal life, but not at that price (18:18–23). The 'rich fool' is so called, not for being rich but for thinking that riches are the aim of life, and neglecting to become 'rich toward God' (12:16–21). The rich man in another parable is condemned to torment, not for his wealth but for his cruel indifference toward the poor man at his gate (16:19–31). But though selfishness and covetousness are more obvious in the rich, they are not more wrong in the rich than in the poor.

The power of wealth to assist others is frequently insisted upon, by the giving of alms, for example (18:22, 12:33, 19:8); by hospitality to the poor (14:12–13; compare 21 'the poor and maimed and blind and lame', where Matthew says only 'as many as you find'); by surrendering your coat, giving to every one who begs from you, doing good, lending, expecting nothing in return (6:29–30, 35). 'You will be blessed because they cannot repay you' (14:14). In such ways wealth may be consecrated to 'provide yourselves with purses that grow not old, with a treasure in the heavens that does not fail, where no thief approaches and no moth destroys' (12:33). A similar point is made in sayings now attached to the parable of the embezzling steward, though probably not originally part of it: 'make friends for yourselves by means of unrighteous mammon, so that when it fails, they may receive you into the eternal habitations' (16:9). Perhaps the most striking affirmation of the spiritual advantages of wealth is the saying of Jesus which only Luke rescued from oblivion — 'It is more blessed to give than to receive' (Acts 20:35).

For all this, wealth can be, and often is, 'unrighteous mammon'. Luke shows how love of it made the rich farmer a bankrupt at the last, the rich ruler abandon the quest for perfection, the rich gourmet end in torment; how wealth lured Zaccheus into dishonesty, and Judas into betrayal. The danger is that wealth is addictive: 'where your treasure is, there will your heart be also' (12:34). That is to say, the heart gravitates to whatever it counts precious, and in the end what you value makes you what you are. So covetousness can ruin character and relationships, inciting brothers to quarrel about inheritance (12:13), or exposing untrustworthiness in spiritual as in material things (16:10–11). The rich so easily forget (or never learn) that 'a man's life does not consist in the abundance of his possessions', which he may so easily lose, and must in the end leave behind, but in more permanent values. Life, in Jesus' eyes, is far more than food, raiment, or investments.

Above all, wealth was a serious hurdle to anyone desiring to enter God's kingdom. 'How hard it is for those who have riches to enter the kingdom of God! For it is easier for a camel to go through the eye of a needle than for a rich man to enter the kingdom . . .' — and the difficulty is no way lessened by fanciful guesses that the 'eye' was a postern gate in Jerusalem, or the 'camel' originally a 'cable'. Familiar with a form of religion which required considerable resources to enable one to keep the law, attend feasts, give alms, offer sacrifices, and the rest, the disciples exclaimed, 'Then who can be saved?' And Jesus answered, recognizing the difficulty. 'What is impossible with men is possible with God' (18:24–27). The story of Zaccheus' conversion from dishonesty, avarice, and greed, to generous righteousness, proves that conclusively.

> Of these sayings on the power and danger of riches, no less than eighteen are preserved by Luke alone. His interest in the theme is further shown by the fact that he alone records the parables of the two debtors, the builder with insufficient capital, and the lost coin; and by his placing together stories of men who used wealth badly, well, or not at all (19:1–27).
>
> Luke's interest is maintained in *Acts*, in the account of Barnabas' great generosity, the early converts' sharing of wealth, the church's concern for her poor, the resulting dishonesty of Ananias and Sapphira, the toil of Paul in independent self-support, the collective gift of the Gentile churches to Judean Christians, and the very significant retort of Peter to Simon Magus: 'Your silver perish with you, because you thought you could obtain the gift of God with money' (Acts 8:20).

The other side of this problem of wealth is of course the problem of poverty. Quite apart from his own upbringing, much in Jesus' teaching reveals his understanding of the difficulties of living on small resources. His lesson on trusting in the Father's provision, his emphasis upon almsgiving, hospitality, generosity, and his own constant concern and friendship for those in need, reveal his sympathy. He understood, too, the costliness, as well as the value, of the small gifts of the poor (21:1–4); and the bitterness of being exploited by the wealthy, when bereavement meant hasty burial, a mortgage upon the home, and early surrender of all to the rapacious lawyer (20:47). Moreover, Jesus shows an uncritical gentleness towards the dying thief, not condoning the thieving, but perhaps understanding its causes. It reveals a sensitive understanding of the feelings of the poor that, in sending out his disciples, he would have them practise living by faith before preaching that lifestyle to others (9:3, 10:4).

Somewhat unexpectedly, Jesus can say (according to Luke alone), 'Blessed are you poor . . . Blessed are you that hunger now, for you shall be satisfied' (6:20–21; Matthew softens to 'poor in spirit'). That the rich find the kingdom hard to enter might imply that the poor find it easier; but in addition, the rich ' have received their consolation', while that of the poor is still to come (6:24). The same thought of a reversal of fortunes occurs in the Magnificat (1:52–53), and in the parable of the rich man and Lazarus: 'Son, remember that you in your lifetime received your good things, and Lazarus in like manner evil things; but now he is comforted here, and you are in anguish' (16:25). The implication appears to be that an over-arching justice operates in the kingdom of God, though the 'riches' that compensate for poverty may not include literal wealth.

But with assurance, Jesus gives also warning, for poverty certainly has spiritual dangers. The thorns that choke the seed of God's word include both the deceitfulness of riches and the cares of this world. The covetousness that poisons the rich with avarice can equally embitter the poor with envy. Jesus was not interested in the transfer of property from one covetous soul to another (12:13–15), and he warned as firmly against anxiety about the lack of *things*, as against confidence in having much.

Both wealth and poverty were for Jesus among the accidents, not the essentials, of life; man's real treasure, 'the pearl of great price', is to live under God's rule. Detachment — the ability to be rich without loving money or growing proud, or to be poor without anxiety or envy — was the way to contentment. Though it must be added again, very clearly, that Jesus never counselled detachment about other people's poverty; the duty of everyone who has is to share, give, lend, feed the hungry, clothe the naked, give hospitality to the homeless.

In preserving and underlining this side of Christ's teaching, Luke is not only demonstrating his own interest in the problem of the unequal distribution of wealth, nor only his own compassion for the poor. He saw in the Christian movement an ideal, a motive, and a power, making for mutual care, and for social justice towards another section of society, and he would have Theophilus know it.

The Force of the Argument

The sinful, the foreigner, the nationalist 'Zealot', the sick, the disadvantaged woman, the poor — each represents a 'social question', and each focusses a special interest of the physician-evangelist as he watches Jesus. Therein lies Luke's particular understanding of Christianity, his vision of Christ, and of the kingdom of God, and his case for a responsible assessment of the church and her work by the leaders of Roman society. In his view, the *moral* evils observed by historians and satirists, and much of the suffering that afflicted many, were *partly* engendered by (and in turn helped to create) *social* evils, which threatened the security of the State and deeply concerned its rulers and officials.

> Roman military leaders, and aspirants to imperial office, were usually taught the Stoic philosophy, to instil obedience, endurance, and responsibility, and to produce a reliable colonial service. As Seneca's training of the emperor Nero shows, the scheme was not always successful, but it did instil social concern in the better men. In addition to self-discipline, Stoicism taught a law of Nature (ordained by a beneficent 'god', hardly thought of as personal, but as 'the soul of all things') before which all were equal, even slaves and women, and virtue and peace were extolled. In Epictetus (contemporary with Luke) Stoicism at its best shared with Christianity love of enemies, brotherhood, equality, freedom, submission, as social virtues. But it was basically academic, cheerless, uncomforting, humanistic, lacked moral resources, and had no redemptive power.

Luke could count upon the immediate interest of a class with this background, when he showed Jesus declaring at the outset that the coming of the Spirit upon him meant good news to the poor, release to the captives, recovery of sight to the blind and liberty for the oppressed. Without any glib assertion that 'Jesus is the solution to all social problems', Luke does demonstrate that Christianity possessed social relevance, promise, and power; that the Christian message could be the answer to the prevalent social malaise, the widespread deprivation and decay. He shows that Christianity bred people with a social conscience, a wide charity, a very human concern for the least, the lowest, and the unlovely, and a broad sympathy with all sorts and conditions of men.

It mattered to Luke's readers that Christianity fostered good citizenship, fairness, cohesiveness, good neighbourliness, and the rehabilitation of the many antagonistic to, or hurt by, society. Luke is suggesting that Jesus could be the saviour of society as well as of sinners — *he wept* (in Luke's Gospel) *over a city that did not know the things that make for social peace.* Rome might well remember that!

All this insight and concern amounted to a *Christian* humanism, essentially human in its appreciation of human needs, its concern and sympathy for human suffering and failure, its support and prayer for every true human ideal and hope. And yet not merely humanistic. For Luke's solution to the world's problems was no sentimental humanitarianism, as though the world could be saved by simple kindness, the balance of competing self-interest, or the 'education of the masses'. Luke documents and describes a divine intervention, in Christ, into the world's affairs, an intervention which made all the difference to the problems, and to the hope of betterment.

For God in Christ was the friend of sinners, aliens, zealots, women, the sick, the poor. In the church, Spirit-filled Christians shared a corporate social conscience, and a divinely-nourished social drive. Their hope was not in man, nor in 'the attainment of human salvation by human resources in accordance with human ideals'. Their present faith and future hope was in the kingdom of God, the inbreaking of a personal power, 'miraculous' in human eyes, in one born of, bearing, and bestowing, the divine Spirit. Into a world bankrupt of truth and energy, Jesus had stepped; and in it, through the church, he was still at work. That is the heart of Luke's message and of his humanism: '*God* has visited and redeemed his people'.

And Luke wants Theophilus and his friends to know that, too.

────── CHAPTER 10 ──────

The Unforgettable Portrait

Although Luke's approach and affirmations are less didactic than Matthew's, less theological than John's, there is no doubt that he found entirely unique significance in the coming, ministry, death and resurrection of Jesus. He says nothing of Jesus' pre-existence, or of incarnation, yet for him Christ's life and death are turning-points of history, and reaction to him determines individual and national destiny. The praise and prophecy that surrounded Christ's birth, the herald who prepared his way, the divine purpose which shaped his career, his own sense of divine sonship and vocation, and the divine witness to him at baptism and transfiguration, confirmed by his resurrection, all emphasize that, in Luke's eyes, Jesus had more than human importance. His total significance was greater even than being born of the Spirit, bearing the Spirit, and bestowing the Spirit, valid and vital though that assessment of him was, in Luke's reconstruction of Christian beginnings.

For Luke, it was more important that we see Jesus clearly than that we follow events of his story in precise order. From this point of view, the long middle section of his Gospel, with its miscellaneous memories, has further value. It provides a series of vignettes illustrating what Jesus was like, how he spoke, acted, responded to challenges, claims or need. The more traditional introductory chapters explain who he was, the equally traditional closing chapters tell what happened to him; but central to the whole is the pen-portrait of a person, the most important person in the world, and in all history. And Luke's picture of him is exceedingly vivid and compelling.

A Man Among Men

Though not the main impression of Jesus in Luke, perhaps the earliest is simply of his humanness. The details of Christ's conception, birth, 'swaddling cloths', his presentation in the temple and circumcision, all set within an aura of peasant home-life and simple relations, create at once this feeling of his oneness with all humanity, as the beginning of everything else. The endearing story of the boyhood escapade in Jerusalem, when, reluctant to cut short what was probably his first holiday in the great city, Jesus stayed behind, and then made every boy's excuse, that his parents should have known where to find him — what boy would not have tried it on? Only Luke tells of it; perhaps only Luke was sufficiently free of theological inhibitions to tell it. And he does not fail to add a very human touch, mentioning the lesson learned: 'he went down with them and came to Nazareth, and was obedient to them . . .' He even adds how his mother remembered that frightening incident, and how Jesus grew wiser with time.

This very human aspect of the portrait is caught again and again throughout the Gospel, in the evident pain and disappointment of his rejection at Nazareth, for example. At first, his neighbours' reaction was favourable: 'all spoke well of him, and wondered at the gracious words which proceeded out of his mouth'. But they added, 'Is not this Joseph's son?', a question which, as Mark shows, expressed 'offence' that he should so speak to people amongst whom he grew up. There is an edge to Jesus' reply, 'Truly I say to you, no prophet is acceptable in his own country . . .', which betrays his own sense of unreasoning hostility and frustration.

We feel that sense again in the lament 'O Jerusalem, Jerusalem, killing the prophets and stoning those who are sent to you! How often would I have gathered your children together as a hen gathers her brood under her wings, and you would not!' (13:34), and in his tears at sight of the city. We are made aware of the inner strain upon his spirit when he voices his desire for companionship (22:15, 40), and the personal sorrow behind his words to the Twelve, 'The hand of him who betrays me is with me on the table'. Even more expressive of inner pain are the words later, 'Judas, would you betray the Son of man with a kiss?'

Gethsemane is an almost total unveiling: the prayer, the need of strengthening, the earnestness and anguish, the sweat copious as blood-drops from a wound, and then the deep loneliness behind the regretful rebuke, 'Why do you sleep?' In a curious way, that scene *both* brings Jesus infinitely near to our weak and stricken humanity, *and* sets him apart, as one who tasted more of its agony than we shall ever understand.

That need of prayer, continuous through the story, at quiet moments as well as crises, on one side of its meaning, also brings Jesus very close to our own dependence and need.

> According to Luke, Jesus prayed at baptism, in a desert place under pressure, in the hills before choosing the Twelve, alone with the disciples, on the mount of transfiguration, at the disciples' return from their mission, 'in a certain place' (so praying as to evoke the disciples' request to be taught to pray), for Simon's coming 'sifting' time, in Gethsemane, and still upon the cross. In addition Jesus provided a pattern for prayer, spoke four parables devoted to prayer, counselled

that men 'pray always', pray against temptation, and — very significantly — ask for the Holy Spirit. (3:21, 5:16, 6:12, 9:18, 29, 10:21, 11:1, 22:32, 41, 44, 24:46; 11:2–13, 18:1–14, 21:36)

Similarly, Jesus' resort to the quiet affection of the home at Bethany reveals a very human craving for support, and his gentle, but sad, understanding of Peter's mingled ardour and weakness (22:31–34) again shows his insight into human failings. But that same gentleness is shown to all weakness, in distressed women, the sick, the outcast, the friendless, the penitent, and to children.

The human characteristic which we in the west most miss in Jesus is humour, as we miss it in most of the Bible. It was not lacking in Jesus, though Luke himself makes little of it, perhaps because of his own temperament, or that of his readers. There is a kind of pun in telling a fisherman, whose night of labour had yielded no 'catch', that henceforth he will 'catch men — alive' (Greek). There is something mildly amusing (that is, literally ridiculous) in the idea of someone trying to remove a speck from his brother's eye all unconscious of the beam of timber (Greek) jutting from his own, round which he peers with difficulty. The image of the fierce and fiery Baptist as a reed trembling at each breath of wind, his camel's hair and leather girdle transformed into the soft raiment and gorgeous apparel of the court dandy, surely raised a smile (7:24–25). The idea of lighting a lamp deliberately to put it under a bed would raise an eyebrow, if it were not so hackneyed now (8:10).

If we could forget all that we ever heard preached, and every commentator we have read, on Martha and Mary, we might be able to appreciate the good humour which poured oil on troubled domestic waters when Jesus said, 'Martha, Martha, you are getting tense and fussy about putting on a spread. One simple course is all we want, and Mary has already chosen her plateful — don't let's take it from her!' The pestilential neighbour who keeps nagging away at the door until he gets what he wants (11:8); the newly married man who early finds he cannot get away any longer to every party he's invited to (14:20); the fairy-tale master who greets his labourers and shepherds with a meal ready, and a cheery welcome (17:7); the lazy judge, nagged into hearing a plea by fear, not of God or man but of a black eye from a woman (18:4–5 Greek), have all come down to us with such an aura of ecclesiastical solemnity that we no longer visualize the crowd listening — and grinning.

The camel struggling through that needle's eye was intended to make fun of an idea. There is something mildly funny, too, despite all the laden meanings, in the figure of Jesus peering up into a sycamore tree to invite the little man, Zaccheus, sitting among the branches, to give him a meal — that is why the children love the story. Probably another pun lies in the words 'If these children (*benim*) were silent the very stones (*banim*) would cry out' (19:40, Aramaic, compare Matthew 3:9). And to wish that 'Jerusalem' ('foundation' or 'possession' of peace) really knew the things that make for peace (19:41), is entirely in line with the ancient prophets' light play upon place-names.

Unfortunately, Luke's earnestness (and our own sanctimonious mood when reading scripture) do not encourage us to recognize lighter touches in the speech of Jesus, sometimes to our serious confusion. For example, Luke seems to have missed the irony (as most of us do) in that otherwise perplexing promise, 'I appoint for you that you may eat and drink at my table in my kingdom, and sit on thrones judging the twelve tribes of Israel' (22:30; Matthew 19:28 makes Jesus say 'on twelve thrones', and the 'promise' an answer to Peter's 'What then shall we have?'). This is so unlike any reward Jesus seriously promised to his followers, whom he was striving to wean from materialist hopes, and it so obviously includes Judas, that it cannot have been intended literally.

Uncertainties apart, the less solemn side of Jesus' teaching, like his quick sympathy with human feeling, makes the human side of Jesus' nature unmistakable in Luke's portrait.

A Forthright Man

Yet this is plainly not the feature that Luke most emphasizes. He underlines an extremely forceful, challenging, almost abrasive quality in Jesus, making him one not to be ignored, certainly not to be trifled with, nor threatened. Even Christ's ordinary speech had a 'tart' flavour, arresting, memorable, and incisive. The fickle religious preferences of the crowd are the antics of fretful children, playing one minute at weddings, the next at funerals, and always unsatisfied (7:31). Voluble wiseacres made a great deal of their ability to read signs of approaching rain, or heat, but could not read the symptoms of the crucial time in which they were living (12:54–56).

For some evil-doers, Jesus prescribes a millstone and the nearest sea; others he describes as making of the temple a thieves' kitchen. He pilloried the self-righteous in a merciless caricature of their praying (18:11–12), and summed up a whole district's opinion of their ruler and his ways in two words — 'that fox . . .' (13:32). He characterized the whole negative thrust of Judaism as a 'sweeping, putting-in-order, spring-cleaning religion', which leaves the house of life a tidy, but vacant, invitation to every passing evil 'squatter' (11:24–26). The worse tyrant a ruler is, the more likely he is to inscribe 'Benefactor' on his coins (22:25). The spiritually enlightened can learn a lot by way of common prudence from the meanest embezzler 'cooking' his master's books (16:1–8).

Much of Jesus' forthrightness was demonstrated in the irony he employed, and the paradoxes he threw into public discussion. 'It would never do for a prophet to perish away from Jerusalem!' (13:33). 'Blessed are you when men hate you . . . exclude you . . . revile you . . . Rejoice in that day, and leap for joy . . .!' (6:22–23). 'So you . . . consent to the deeds of your fathers; they killed (the prophets), and you build their tombs!' (11:48). So too, 'Blessed are you poor . . . you that hunger . . . you that weep . . . Woe to you that laugh . . .' (6:20–25) are paradoxes intended to startle thought. So are 'Love your enemies . . .', 'To him who strikes you on the cheek, offer the other . . .', 'Give to every one who begs from you . . . If any one does not hate . . . he cannot be my disciple' (6:27–30, 14:26). So Jesus discouraged impulsiveness with a peremptory 'Count the cost . . . Leave the dead to bury their own dead . . . No one who looks back is fit . . .' (14:28, 9:60–61).

Sometimes Christ's unanswerable logic quells criticism. Answering the charge that his exorcisms were achieved by Satan's help, he asked, 'If Satan . . . is divided against himself, how will his kingdom stand? . . . If I cast out demons by Beelzebul, by whom do your sons cast them out?' Defending the disciples against blame for not observing a fast, Jesus asked, 'Can you make wedding guests fast before the bridegroom has left the table?' And to Sadducees, who accepted only *Genesis* to *Deuteronomy* as scripture and denied any resurrection, Jesus asserted, apparently to everyone's surprise, 'That the dead are raised, even Moses showed . . . where he calls the Lord the God of Abraham . . . Isaac . . . Jacob. Now he is not the God of the dead but of the living . . .' (20:37–38).

Again, Jesus could shock sometimes by his uncompromising realism. That gallery of rogues presented in the parables suggested this; and so does his unequivocal declaration about the cost of discipleship, a daily cross, willingness to lose one's life. So again does his warning that some who claim acquaintance with Christ will be turned away as unrecognized (13:26). Jesus had an unsentimental mind. When some pious romantic contributed to the dining-table conversation the sententious remark, 'Blessed is he who shall eat bread in the kingdom of God!', Jesus replied with the parable of the great banquet to which those invited 'all alike began to make excuses' — and stupid ones! 'Blessed is the womb that bore you . . .' called an effusive woman after him; '*But* he said, "Blessed rather are those who hear the word of God and keep it!"' (11:27–28).

Such blunt speech made Jesus immune to flattery. The conventional, thoughtless 'Good teacher . . .' was brought up short with 'Why do you call me good? No one is "good" but God alone' (18:18–19). The fawning fourfold commendation, that he spoke and taught rightly, showed no partiality, truly taught the way of God, which introduced the trick question about paying tribute to Caesar, is sharply brushed aside with 'Show me a coin', for he 'perceived their craftiness'. The same blunt realism made Jesus dismiss almost curtly mere theoretical questions. 'Lord, will those who are saved be few?' was answered with 'You strive to enter . . .!' (13:23). The question about certain Galileans whom Pilate murdered, and another eighteen on whom a tower fell, 'Do you think they were worse sinners than all others . . . ?' was dismissed with 'No, but unless you repent you will perish!'

But the prevailing note of Jesus' speech, in *all* circumstances, was authority. The common people exclaimed at it, religious leaders challenged it, unclean spirits, wind, and sea, 'obeyed' it, a military commander testified to it eloquently; some said that Elijah (the prophet that 'troubled Israel') had returned, others that John the Baptist had risen from the dead, so forcefully did Jesus speak (4:32, 36, 5:24, 7:7, 20:1, 8; 9:8). When that authority turned to rebuke it could be severe, silencing the demon-possessed, dismissing the mere suggestion that he punish the Samaritans, warning the Galilean towns which rejected his ministry that the judgement will be more tolerable for Tyre and Sodom than for them.

Occasionally, rebuke boiled over into indignation. When that 'woman of the city' gatecrashed the wealthy Pharisee's house, and amid a crowded courtyard wept over Christ's feet, Jesus met head-on the look of contempt he caught on the Pharisee's face, and his muttered comment. Quietly Jesus told a story about two debtors, and extracted from his host the admission that great forgiveness evoked great love. Then suddenly Jesus launched into a blistering contrast, point by point, between the passionate courtesies this woman had shown him — her tears the water, her hair the towel, her ointment the oil, her kisses for his feet the welcome — making up for the graceless omissions of the proud Pharisee. And all this said in the presence of his gaping neighbours (7:36–50)!

The village would remember that outburst, as the disciples would remember his indignation at their failure at the foot of the mount of transfiguration (9:41). And as others would remember one sabbath in the synagogue, when, faced with the man with the withered hand and a ring of scribes and Pharisees watching eagerly to see if 'they might find an occasion against him', Jesus roundly demanded whether it was right on the sabbath to do good — as he proposed to do — or to kill — as they were plotting to do! His indignation was matched by their 'fury' (6:6–11). Equally memorable was the service in which Jesus released the stooping woman, and publicly pilloried the inconsistency of his critics, who would readily release their own ox or ass on the sabbath for watering.

In yet another synagogue service Jesus challenged the lawyers, the presiding elder, the 'godly' leaders of the community, 'Which is easier, to say "Your sins are forgiven you" or to say "Rise and walk"?', and while they pondered, unwilling to admit he could do either, Jesus acted. The claim to forgive was easy to make, since none could refute it; the command to walk required visible evidence to justify it. But further, both the patient and the congregation assumed that, paralysis being due to sin, forgiveness must precede healing. The man's recovery would (in their minds) prove he had been forgiven. Jesus commanded the man to rise, take up his mattress, and go home. The man did so, and the whole district was dumbfounded (5:17–26).

These public attacks upon 'authority' (compare 11:39, 42–44, 46, 52, 12:1, 20:45–46) were often devastating, just because the delighted spectators recognized how truly Jesus described the leaders' ways. A more extended attack, which took a favourite passage of Isaiah, describing God's care for the sacred vineyard of Israel, and showed how the tenants had, through the centuries, withheld God's due proportion of the fruits, led on to two 'outrageous' affirmations: the vineyard would be taken from Israel and given to others; the professedly expert builders of God's house had got it all wrong! It is scarcely surprising that the scribes and priests saw his point, and decided this could not go on. They attempted at once to arrest him (20:9–19). His attacks upon some of the rich (16:19–31, 14:12–14, for example) were equally dangerous; so was his scathing comment when at last they arrested him, in secrecy, at night: 'This is the hour you would choose, for so dark a deed!' (22:52–53).

It must be added that Jesus was sometimes deliberately provocative. Was it tactful to introduce the Syrian Naaman, or the widow of alien Zarephath, into a synagogue sermon in a racially sensitive district? Or to intrude the same racist issue into his answer to the simple question, 'Who is my neighbour?' by making his example a Samaritan? Or, for that matter, to draw attention to the fact that of ten lepers cleansed, the only one grateful enough, or with the good manners, to return and give thanks was — 'this foreigner', a Samaritan (17:16, 18)?

To praise a Roman's faith, did he need to contrast Israel's unbelief? To highlight his generation's impenitence, need Jesus cite, offensively, hated Nineveh, proud Tyre, despised Sodom, the pagan Queen of Sheba, as models? And would it not sound somewhat lacking in respect to ask a group of Pharisees, publicly, when they cited the law against him, 'Have you not read . . .?' (6:3)!

Sharpness, irony, paradox, logic, realism, forthrightness, authority, indignation, challenge, provocation: whether or not this amounts to 'abrasiveness', the speech of Jesus was hardly to be ignored. It is necessary to spell this out, and to illustrate it fully, because the prevailing image of Jesus for so long has been of one wholly soft-spoken, sentimental, inoffensive, even effeminate. Yet there is no doubt whatever that Jesus had 'a rough edge' to his tongue. His antagonists often 'marvelled' or were 'silenced', reacted with 'awe' or 'fear', 'no longer dared to ask', or 'were put to shame' (5:26, 9:45, 7:16, 13:17, 14:4, 20:26, 40). These are not normal reactions to a gentle-voiced, winsome charmer!

The Complete Human

But Jesus' bold and determined actions matched the boldness of his speech. As he strode towards Jerusalem, determination in every stride (9:51); as he stood fearless before a madman whose violence had necessitated chains, and driven him forth of society to live amongst tombs (8:26); and as he walked unharmed through a hostile crowd, all urging that he be lynched, but each afraid to touch him (4:30), Jesus was demonstrating exactly that quality of manly composure that would appeal directly to Luke's readers. Roman officials and military leaders would understand exactly what self-command such crises of danger required. In the garden of Gethsemane, when violence suddenly flashed, Jesus showed again the same promptness and command.

Ruefully, perhaps, Roman readers would notice how Jesus outwitted both Jews and Romans as he made his final challenge to Jerusalem. For Jesus made apt use of the usual welcome sung to pilgrims coming to the great religious festivals — 'Blessed be the king who comes in the name of the Lord! Peace in heaven and glory in the highest!', chanted amidst waving branches called 'Hosannas' (compare Psalm 118:19–27). So Jesus rode into the city, surrounded by just such shouted praise, so that some Pharisees, who perceived the effect, told him to silence his followers. Yet nothing in the scene could be reported to the Roman authorities as seditious; a carpenter on a donkey amid peasants getting religiously excited, posed no threat to Caesar!

Later, we note the way Jesus contrived to reach the Upper Room in Jerusalem which he had already reserved for the last supper, in a city of enemies. The two disciples who were led to the house were separated from those who might, unwittingly or deliberately, reveal where they were going, until Jesus was quite ready (22:8–14).

Jesus' reply to the warning that Herod desired to kill him bears all the marks of the 'Stoical', self-possessed, unflinching character that Romans admired. 'Go and tell that fox, "Behold, I cast out demons and perform cures today and tomorrow, and the third day I will finish my course. Nevertheless I must go on my way today and tomorrow and the day following; for it cannot be that a prophet should perish away from Jerusalem".' In other words, Jesus will adhere to his own plans and mission until his work is done, Herod or no Herod; when he is ready he will leave Herod's domains for Jerusalem, but not because of any threat from the king. Jesus is his own master, wholly impervious to pressure.

And so throughout his ministry, as in speech so in action, Jesus was uncompromising, fearless, avoiding no confrontation where truth and principle were at stake, ready to initiate situations of disagreement or danger, if his work required it. A true man, as the Romans would think, manly, purposeful, undeterred, courageous, not to be intimidated or deflected from his purpose. And as he lived, so he died. Throughout his trial Jesus had remained dignified and self-possessed, neither railing back when the Jews 'vehemently' accused him, nor offering excuses or pleading for mercy from Pilate; accepting the soldiers' coarseness and the physical agony of crucifixion without blazing resentment, curses, or whining. And, at the last, 'Jesus, crying with a loud voice, said "Father, into thy hands I commit my spirit!" And having said this, he breathed his last.' And when the centurion, who had been in charge of Jesus throughout, saw what had taken place, 'he praised God, and said, "Certainly this man was innocent!"' (23:46–47). That centurion was of the same culture, background, and training, as Luke's intended readers. He recognized a true *man* when he met one.

Even so, Christ's 'manliness' is only part of the matchless portrait. Even that had a vulnerable side, a capacity for deep feeling (22:41, 44), that some Romans would consider more characteristic of women than of men. But in truth, man and woman are not opposites but complementary. Full humanity embraces both the forms of man which God created. The exclusively masculine man is as unbalanced as the effeminate man, and human nature, as we reverence it in Christ, combines in perfect balance varying qualities that make him the ideal alike of men and women.

Christ's was not the arrogant maleness that treats women with contempt, or with superior tolerance. Behind his ministry to women lay an evident *rapport* with woman's thought and feeling. He really understood the frustration of the widow clamouring for a hearing by a lazy judge; the panic of a woman who had mislaid a bridal heirloom. He truly *felt* the contempt poured upon the woman in the Pharisee's house; he grieved with the desperate sense of loss that afflicted the widow of Nain (compare 2:37, 7:12, 18:3, 20:47, 21:2; Christ's mother was probably widowed). Jesus even shared the waking bewilderment of Jairus' young daughter, and spoke and acted as though she were merely waking from sleep. Even yet we do not know if she was really dead (see 8:52); neither did she.

And women understood Jesus, more quickly and more deeply than did the men about him, who continued to quarrel over precedence while his heart suffered. Certainly Martha and Mary understood his need, and the woman in the house of Simon understood his meaning. Certain women of Jerusalem bewailed and lamented his fate, when the men were merely fearful for their own safety; and women remained to the last at the cross (23:55). Women came first to the tomb (24:10–11), while the men were still frightened, and arguing. (And it is not an entirely foolish speculation that one of the two disciples walking to Emmaus was a woman; the *subject* throughout 23:55–24:12 is 'the women', and while there could be a change at 24:13, because the men have just been mentioned, Luke does not indicate it. We know that Mary, the wife of one of them, Cleopas — 24:18 — had lingered at the cross, according to John 19:25; and we may ask, as others have done, 'Who else should a Christian man be walking home with on a Sunday night, but with his wife?')

It might be invidious to suggest that Jesus knew the tendency of women to keep pestering until they succeed (18:3); to look back at things familiar when fearful of change (17:32); to be persistent and practical when men are most useless (23:55–24:1); how they must do their grinding *together* (17:35); and share good news with the people next door (15:9). It is but factual to remark how much Jesus knew of patching garments and storing wine (5:36–38; Mark appears to have understood this saying better than Luke did: see Mark 2:21); of baking bread; of washing up (11:37); the problems created by sudden demands for hospitality (11:5–6); the effect of leaven (12:1); the tension that can arise between sisters (12:53). Jesus understood, too, the piety that brought a widow deep satisfaction in giving what she could, small though it was (21:2). He showed, moreover, an interest in children that is natural to most women but which some men lack — an interest observant (7:32), appreciating (9:47), defending (17:2), welcoming (18:15), fearful for their future (19:44, 23:28). He appears twice to speak of the people of Jerusalem as 'children' in their simplicity and danger, in what can only be called a 'motherly' way (13:34, 19:42).

Relevant here is the quick, keen sympathy of Jesus, with that bowed woman, for example, for whom he had, beside release, a caressing hand, a stong defensive word, and a memorable phrase of dignity, 'daughter of Abraham' — what depth of insight that reveals! His solitary word (in Luke) about divorce sees the damage done only from the woman's viewpoint (16:18). His personal word and greeting for the woman in the crowd, too shy and 'trembling' to confront him, shows the same intuitive reading of more than physical need. And his quick word of reassurance to a distraught father has the same swift awareness of another's feeling that marks a woman's sympathy oftener than a man's (8:50). The coming days of 'vengeance', which Jesus foresees will fall upon Jerusalem, will bear most hardly upon the women, especially on those with young children about them, and on expectant and nursing mothers. It is surprising to hear a *man* say that they will bitterly regret their motherhood, in those days (21:23, 23:28–30).

This intuitive understanding of people 'from the inside' is more usual in women than in men; and so is the preoccupation with personal situations and relationships in preference to abstract and hypothetical questions. Few women would have much patience with theoretical puzzles like 'How many shall be saved?' or, 'Are people who have accidents greater sinners than other people?' or, 'Is it lawful to practise medicine on the sabbath day?' or, 'Is it lawful to chew corn on your sabbath walk ?' Nor had Jesus. He too reduced each question to the personal issue of the enquirer's own position, the patient's need, the hunger of the walkers, where many men would have indulged in interminable debate.

All this is saying no more than that, when the character of Jesus is analysed in detail, and his strength and tenderness, forthrightness and gentle insight, are fully described, the unity in one character of mainly 'masculine' and mainly 'feminine' moral traits is unmistakable. That is why he is the ideal of that moral humanity in which manhood and womanhood alike can find their goal — and have done so. His moral perfection lies in the unique balance of complementary virtues; their harmony lends to his whole life its completeness and poise, the 'measure of the stature of the fullness of Christ'. He is the complete human, appealing as strongly to feminine love and devotion as to masculine obedience and loyalty.

All in all, Luke has portrayed for us a real man, genuinely human if not *only* human, and he has placed him firmly on the human scene, and within the stream of human history, by those definitive dates and places (1:5, 26, 39, 2:1–4, 3:1–3). If the church has distorted the portrait into that of a soft effeminate 'saint', always wearing a half-concealed halo, and altogether too good and gentle for this rough world, that is not Luke's fault. In *Luke*, Jesus is forceful, strong, clever, dangerous, not to be browbeaten or ignored, but only obeyed or crucified. But he is also much, much more.

More than Human

That something more than human is on foot in the ministry of Jesus is evident, of course, from the authority of his words, the power of his deeds, and the fact of his resurrection. Men expressed some sense of this as they watched and listened: 'They were all amazed and said . . . "What is this word? for with authority and power he commands the unclean spirits and they come out" . . . Amazement seized them all, and they glorified God and were filled with awe, saying, "We have seen strange things today" . . . The crowd sought to touch him, for power came forth from him . . . "Who then is this, that he commands even wind and water, and they obey him?" . . . All were astonished at the majesty of God' (4:36, 5:26, 6:19, 8:25, 9:43). Four times that 'something more than human' is described as a 'visitation' (by Zechariah looking forward 1:68, 78 Greek; by 'a great crowd' 7:16; by Jesus himself 19:44). God's 'visiting' his people, or his enemies, is the usual word (over seventy times) in the Old Testament for divine intervention, whether to bless, give children, or harvest, to rescue, in gracious favour, or most frequently in punishment, 'visiting iniquity . . .' God's intervention in Jesus was to redeem (1:68), to demonstrate power (7:16), to offer opportunity (19:44).

For Jesus, that divine intervention through him as agent involved life under continual compulsion. Jesus 'must' preach the kingdom ('I was sent for this purpose'), heal, suffer many things, go on his way, be rejected, be numbered with transgressors, be delivered up and crucified, suffer and enter his glory (4:43, 9:22, 13:16 Greek, 13:33, 17:25, 22:37, 24:7, 26–27, 44, compare 2:49). Every life that counts for anything experiences this compulsion; with Jesus it evidently intensified towards the end, so that even death itself was something he must 'accomplish' (9:31, 18:31).

This compelling sense of commission had two sides. In three references to it, emphatic mention is made of the course mapped out for Christ in 'what is written . . . in the law of Moses and the prophets and the Psalms . . . in all the scriptures'; in particular, Luke's Gospel seven times echoes prophecies of Isaiah. The effect is to establish that the appearance of Jesus was in the divine purpose; that his universal mission, his offer of salvation, his election by God, the gracious nature of the kingdom which he inaugurates, his being reckoned with transgressors, and his suffering their fate, were all foreseen, foretold, and now fulfilled. His life was planned.

The complement to prophecy, in directing Christ's career, was the divine side of that constant prayer-life already noticed. Not only did Jesus renew his inner resources by prayer, he also listened for, and received, the guidance of the Father. Unlike the Pharisees, who 'rejected the purpose of God for themselves' (7:30, a significant phrase), Jesus welcomed the divine control of all he said, did, and suffered. He was not helplessly but willingly obedient (22:22). Even in the anguish of Gethsemane the orientation of his inner life holds true: 'Father, if thou art willing . . . nevertheless not my will, but thine, be done.'

This is extremely important. As God's agent in the establishing of his kingdom on earth, this forceful, independent-minded Man lives under divine direction at every point, moving and acting under divine compulsion. *So he illustrates, and demonstrates, the essential meaning of the kingdom, as living under God's reign day by day.* What is done is God's doing; what is said is God's word; what is offered is God's grace and presence; what is suffered is the cost, in a sinful world, of bringing men to God.

The nearest that Luke comes to describing *incarnation* is that picture of Jesus born by the Spirit's operation, bearing throughout his ministry the endowment of the Spirit, and bestowing the Spirit in the end upon his followers. Luke (and his readers) were probably less theologically inclined than some New Testament writers and readers, and he is satisfied with the titles already given to Jesus in the apostolic church — titles which had gained weight of meaning through nearly fifty years of Christian reflection.

Thus everywhere in his own summaries and statements, Luke uses for Jesus the title he heard constantly in the church, 'Lord' (as Mark also does, once or twice). The word is occasionally used in addressing Jesus by bystanders, questioners, enquirers, meaning no more than 'Sir', a little more deferential than 'Teacher' but with no theological significance (7:6, 9:59, 61, 13:23, 19:8, 25). From personal friends the word might carry more reverence (from Martha 10:40, the disciples 11:1, 24:34, from Peter 5:8, 12:41). But, when Luke himself wishes to tell something Jesus said or did, he usually employs 'the Lord' (7:13, 19, 10:1, 41, 12:42, 13:15, 17:5, 18:6, 19:8); his alternatives are 'Jesus', or just 'he'.

We know that in the apostolic church this title affirmed Christ's absolute superiority and supremacy, practically transferring to Jesus the 'lordship' of the slave-owner over his purchased slave, of Caesar over the whole empire, and of God over the world — for 'Lord' was the word commonly used for 'God' in the Greek Old Testament. This last use of the title, with divine overtones, yet now applied to Jesus, is no exaggeration; for Luke himself so uses it for God, at least ten times (1:16, 2:22–23, 4:8, 12, 18, 5:17, 10:2, 21, 27). This far-reaching use of the same title for God and for Jesus confirms the theological implication elsewhere in *Luke*, that Jesus belongs, essentially, rather to God's side of the divide-human divide than to ours.

The very frequent use of 'prophet' is an acknowledgement of direct divine inspiration and authority in Jesus. A group of messianic titles — 'the Christ' (2:11, 4:41, 9:20, 'Christ a king' 23:2), 'Son of David' (18:38, note 20:41–42), and 'Son of man', a familiar term which Luke uses twenty-two times (four times referring to Christ's death, seven times to his coming glory) — shows Luke keeping close to the Jewish terminology of the original tradition, while the whole messianic idea is transformed by Christ's teaching. This is strikingly confirmed by Luke's always using 'Son of man' as Christ's name for himself. Though its use in Daniel 7, and in the apocryphal 1 Enoch, gave to the phrase for many ears vaguely messianic overtones, yet the *literal* meaning (as in Psalm 8 and many times in *Ezekiel*) was simply 'man'. Jesus let his hearers make of it whatever their insight suggested.

'The holy One of God' (4:34, compare Acts 3:14, John 6:69) may mean consecrated to God, equivalent to 'anointed' or 'consecrated' (as by oil) to

God's service — that is, 'Christ'. Or, as coming from one possessed by 'the spirit of an unclean demon', it may well mean 'the One immaculately holy, and from God'. The 'beloved Son' in whom God is 'well pleased' (3:22, note margin, 20:13; compare Psalm 2:7, Isaiah 42:1 speaking of 'the Servant of the Lord') combines the idea of Messiah with that of the 'Servant' whom Isaiah promised should come, and should suffer. The same meaning is present in 22:27, and the title in 9:35, 23:35.

But 'beloved Son' obviously points towards more than messianic status. So does 'Son of God' (1:32 'Son of the Most High', 1:35, 4:3, 9, 41, 8:28 'Son of the Most High God', 9:35, 22:70). If it is wrong to read into 'Son of God' the theological reflection of later centuries, and of the great church creeds (and the use of the same phrase for Adam 3:38, and as equivalent to 'Christ' 4:41, should make us careful), it is equally wrong to ignore the title's implications — a uniquely intimate relation to God, and an unquestionably divine origin. 'Son of God' can hardly mean less than that.

Luke nowhere explains these titles, but he preserves the startling claim of Jesus to be the one who *alone* truly knows God, and who *alone* can truthfully reveal him to whom he chooses (10:21–22). For Luke, the life, the work and gifts of Christ sufficiently explain what Christians said about him, and we should probably look less for theological definitions than for personal testimony. The Christians whom Luke knew had felt in Christ, and had come to possess in themselves, a truly divine energy and grace. *God had invaded the human scene* — of that Luke was sure — with truth, power, healing, blessing, forgiveness. That invasion of divine energies was personal, not magic, or mere 'influence'; and Jesus was its vehicle, its agent, its exemplar and embodiment, and its channel into other lives. That is why Jesus was unique, indispensable, divine. In him God 'visited and redeemed' all who would receive him. Later philosophy might analyse, argue, and define: what mattered to Luke and to his readers was the experience. They *knew* that Jesus was the Son of God.

So Luke offers to Theophilus and his colleagues a rich portrait of the Founder of the church they knew, as Luke had learned of him from the Christians he had met and the enquiries he had made. This was Jesus, the strong, forthright, fearless leader; the gentle, sympathetic friend of all men and women, with exquisite insight and deep feeling; a saviour of individuals and of society; embodying in himself and offering to others the limitless grace of God Most High.

CHAPTER 11

The Gospel, According to Luke

For some four centuries, the first part of the New Testament was called 'the Gospel', and regarded as one Gospel in four versions, the common tradition about Jesus culled from the corporate recollection of the church, as it filtered through four different minds. Luke's is the cultured Gentile's version, designed to commend Christ and the church to the Graeco-Roman world. In consequence, his account of Jesus is markedly different from those of Matthew, Mark, and John. For many, this will be a surprising conclusion, and we look again at the process which brought it about because it raises some questions urgently relevant to our problems today.

Transplanting the Gospel

For one thing, Luke has translated and transplanted the gospel from one culture to another. Christianity was born out of Judaism, and Matthew continually reminds us of the fact. He uses much Jewish language, which he can assume his readers will understand — 'the bread of the Presence', 'phylacteries', 'binding and loosing', 'God's people', 'tithing', and much else. He quotes very detailed prophecies from the Old Testament, mere phrases like 'He shall be called a Nazarene', 'Out of Egypt have I called my son', which only those very familiar with the Jewish scriptures would recognize. Luke uses only so much of this language as is necessary to keep the story historically accurate without embarrassing his Gentile readers.

More important, whereas Matthew emphasizes strongly the close connection of Christ and Christianity with the Jewish past, as its culmination and fulfilment, Luke — so to speak — detaches the Christian movement from Jewish history, as far as possible, and sets Jesus on the world's stage. Judaism, and a pious Jewish home, are still of course the setting of Jesus' life story, but one hardly needs to know more than that to understand Luke's Jesus. Concepts like 'Messiah', 'messianic kingdom', 'the Son of man' (whom many expected to appear on the clouds), sacrificial worship, Jewish nationalism, legalist religion, and much more, do appear in Luke's story, yet the Messiah, the kingdom, the worship, and the law of God, are all very different from anything Judaism contended for, and anticipated.

Then, as we have seen, Luke has shown great skill in selecting for emphasis precisely those aspects of Jesus' character, those qualities in the Christians he describes, and those elements in the story, such as the appearance of Gentiles, and Pilate's repeated acquittal of Jesus, which his Roman readers would find persuasive. Aspects of Jesus' ministry which would have less appeal to Gentile readers, like his appearance as a great rabbi re-interpreting Jewish law, Luke simply omits.

Obvious though this is, it is possible to miss the profound significance of the process. Luke has not only transplanted Christianity, *so far as possible*, into Gentile terms and Gentile culture; he has detached Christianity from its matrix in Israel's history, Old Testament religion, and Jewish assumptions, prejudices, and hopes, so that Gentile enquirers (like Theophilus) have neither to become Jews, nor to retrace the long preparation for Christ in Judaism, in order to become Christians.

Luke was pre-eminently fitted to help Christianity make this transition out of Jewry into the wider world of his own culture, because his own Christian experience was rooted within, and shaped by, churches far beyond Palestine. And the heart of Christianity is not an historical tradition, but the experience of God in Christ. Luke first encountered that experience in and through the church, learned that its origin, illumination, and sustaining lay in 'the Spirit of Jesus', and then thought and enquired his way back to the gospel-story. High conceptions of God, and high ideals of morality, were involved, some of them inherited from Judaism; and high, constraining loyalty to a remembered story, its central Figure, and a lofty ideal. But the living experience of daily fellowship with God and direction by God, in all the vicissitudes of life, was at its heart, giving relevance and value to all else.

So the *datum* of the Christian gospel is the Spirit-filled, alive, joyous, serving, Christlike church of transformed people. The spoken or written gospel is the explanation of that, a formulation of its inner truth and memories, which we offer to people envious of the quality, the enjoyment, and the social value, of the Christian lifestyle. It follows that, the experience being shared, the explanation of the experience can be formulated, told and retold in any language, partially reformulated to accommodate to new cultures, transferred across centuries of change and continents of alien tradition, and still make its impact, still attract new adherents.

No one, who knows anything of the story of twentieth-century New Testament studies, can miss the parallel between Luke's achievement and our own age's perpetual endeavour to detach what is timeless and unchangeable in Christianity from what belonged simply to its first-century formulation. The need persists, to translate the eternal truth into changing language, to transplant the heart of the gospel into the thought-forms and cultural patterns of each new age; and Luke was the forerunner, and exemplar, in that demanding and somewhat dangerous enterprise.

For the experience must remain Christian, utterly loyal to Christ's insights and revelation, true to his ideal and vision, dependent upon his Spirit, nourished by his teaching and memory, constantly renewed by his forgiveness and grace. That is why Luke lifts Jesus out of his Judaist and Palestine setting and Old Testament background, to be Lord of men's minds and hearts in new circumstances and a new generation. Of course a full understanding of Christianity's background and development requires a knowledge of what went before; Luke himself supplies a résumé of Israel's history in the 'flash-back' of Stephen's speech, and in certain sermons of Paul. Of course Christianity has been immeasurably enriched by drawing upon the treasures of biography, prophetic inspiration, and devotional poetry in the Old Testament, and Luke selectively uses those sources to embellish his own pages. But Christian use of the Old Testament has not always been discriminating, and its influence upon Christian thought has not always been good.

If Luke's contribution to the New Testament had been better appreciated, and the church had looked back over the pre-Christian centuries with gratitude but taking to itself only what was entirely consonant with the new spirit of Jesus, Christian historians would have less to apologize for and explain away. Some of the church's most tragic mistakes and distorted ideals arose from a too close adherence to Jewish presuppositions — the burning of witches, the 'holy war' of extermination, the State-controlled church, the Inquisition, find whatever scriptural justification is conceivable for them in the Old Testament, not the New, and certainly not in the Gospels. Luke clearly understood that, though arising out of Judaism, Christianity had to break free from the religion within which Jesus had been crucified, and address itself in new terms to a new culture and environment. It is a great pity the church did not always understand it too.

The process of transplanting, of discerning what can be changed without loss, what reworded without distortion, what left behind without disloyalty, is extremely delicate, painful, and divisive. But in our rapidly changing world, our increasingly inter-racial and inter-religious society, our emerging multi-cultural, global-village view of the world, could any task be more urgent upon the Christian conscience? Luke has shown it can be done.

Enhancement of Life

Luke's description of the apostolic experience of Christ is unrivalled, exciting, many-sided. The only phrase which might summarize at all adequately the impact of the Lukan Jesus on those who believe would be, 'the total enrichment and enhancement of life in an otherwise grim world'. If the answer of the Stoic to the harshness of life was self-command, discipline, the repression of emotion and the refusal to admit pain, the answer of the Christian as Luke expressed it was an invigoration, an exhilaration of spirit, a moral transformation, a resilience and buoyancy that sprang from a sense of being healed, enlightened, strengthened, opened up to the creative, liberating experience of the grace of God. A radiant faith, a convinced hope, and remarkable courage and boldness in adversity, marked the Christians Luke knew, who yet contrived to sustain humility, generosity, and deep sympathy with others.

> This is much more than a question of terminology, but in fact the words Luke uses for Saviour, save, salvation, derive from a root-word implying preservation or recovery from harm, danger, disease, suffering, death. Its common use was for restoration to health (Asclepius, the god of healing, was entitled *Saviour* for this reason). In his Gospel, Luke speaks of salvation as deliverance from enemies into security, from slavery into liberty, as rehabilitation in character and society (Zaccheus); and, in religious or spiritual connection, as a restoration to healthy existence, within God's kingdom (18:26), from sinfulness (7:50), through forgiveness and light (1:77, 2:30). Where its precise meaning is indicated at all in *Acts*, these meanings recur, plus deliverance from shipwreck, from the influence of an evil generation, cleansing of the heart (15:9, 11), the gift of the Spirit, and a way — and word — of salvation.

The whole tone and emphasis of Luke's language about salvation is thus positive, and life-promoting. It implies a 'healthful' existence, with security, freedom, cleanness, physical and spiritual health, mental soundness, the Spirit's power. It implies, too, forgiveness for past guilt, though this is by no means the central or exclusive idea in salvation, in Luke's thought. Luke has a strong sense of the privilege enjoyed by disciples: 'Among those born of women none is greater than John; yet he who is least in the kingdom of God is greater than he . . . Blessed are the eyes which see what you see! For I tell you that many prophets and kings desired to see what you see, and did not see it, and to hear what you hear, and did not hear it' (7:28, 10:23). The days of Jesus were days of invitation, of opportunity, of feasting and new wine, of fulfilment, so that even the Baptist, who expected axe and fire, winnowing fork and threshing, was perplexed over Jesus' style of ministry (7:18–20).

This is why, in Luke, what Jesus brings is everywhere 'good news' — that emphasis is unmistakable (1:19, 2:10, 3:18, 4:18, 43, 7:22, 8:1, 9:6 Greek, 16:16, 20:1 Greek). Zechariah's description of Christ's ministry anticipates salvation, tender mercy, the dawning day, light, guidance, and peace.

Christ's own summary for John included healings, exorcisms, curing of blindness, lameness, leprosy, deafness, raising the dead, and good news to the poor, a comprehensive enhancement of life-experience for different types of people. Christ's manifesto at Nazareth set out Christ's programme in similar terms, as a year of the Lord's favour, spelling out a prospect which even the most desperate of 'life's broken victims' would find 'good news'.

If Christ's miracles were not all too familiar, now, to stir our wonder, we should feel the positive implication of each one: life again for the widow's son, fuller life for the woman whose life was draining away, a whole life to a 'dead' child; liberty and uprightness for the bowed; freedom to the paralysed, and the dropsical; cleansing and social relationships again, to the lepers; employment for the man whose hand was withered, and with it independence; light for the darkened, calm to the fevered, healing to the suicidal epileptic; speech to the dumb and hearing to the deaf, ushering both into renewed conversation and laughter; sanity to the deranged, deliverance for the possessed, food for the hungry — we may puzzle for ever about *how* it all was done, but not at all about *why*. In every instance where Christ exercised his power for individuals it was to liberate, restore, impart life, bring back light, colour, richness, freedom, fellowship, dignity and hope.

Even the phrases that close the miracle-stories are often eloquent of their purpose, to re-establish the reign of God in areas of experience where evil has disrupted the divine order, and to open doors to enjoyment and opportunity. 'Woman, you are freed . . . And all the people rejoiced at all the glorious things that were done by him . . . Rise and go your way, your faith has made you well . . . The dumb man spoke, and the people marvelled . . . The fever left her, and immediately she rose and served them . . . Go into peace . . . Child, arise . . . Stretch out your hand . . . Jesus gave him back to his father . . . He received his sight and followed him, glorifying God . . . All ate and were satisfied . . . They found the man sitting at the feet of Jesus, clothed, and in his right mind.'

In such expressions, Christ's positive promotion and intensification of *life* at its highest, richest, fullest, and best, is revealed as the meaning of salvation. Repentance, cleansing, forgiveness of sin, have their place, but these are, in Luke's presentation, but preliminary, preparatory, mere clearing of the ground, for what Christ wants to make of life, for all who will.

The final proof of this lies in something else again. It has often been remarked that Luke's is the happiest of the Gospels. It almost opens with 'My spirit rejoices in God, my Saviour', ends with the disciples returning to Jerusalem 'with great joy . . . blessing God', and maintains that note all through. Outbursts of thanksgiving, song, and praise surround the infant Christ. There are more happy scenes in Luke's pages than in the other

Gospels, scenes of childhood, home, youth, health, gladness, swift feet and burning hearts, 'music, making merry, dancing' (15:24–25), all illustrating the angel's promise of 'good news of a great joy . . . to all people'. Luke 6:21 is the only promise in the Gospels that men 'shall laugh'. To obtain a correct impression, however, it is necessary to follow joy through Luke's Gospel, from 1:14 — 'You will have joy and gladness . . . The babe leaped in my womb for joy . . . my spirit rejoices . . . her neighbours and kinsfolk rejoiced with Elizabeth . . . A great joy to all people . . . Rejoice in that day, and leap for joy . . . They receive the word with joy . . . The seventy returned with joy . . . Rejoice that your names are written in heaven . . . Jesus rejoiced in the Holy Spirit . . . All the people rejoiced . . . He lays it on his shoulders rejoicing . . . Rejoice with me . . . more joy in heaven over one sinner who repents . . . Rejoice with me, I have found the coin . . . Joy before the angels of God . . . They began to make merry . . . music and dancing . . . fitting to make merry and be glad . . . (Zaccheus) received him joyfully . . . the whole multitude began to rejoice . . . They still disbelieved for joy . . . They returned to Jerusalem with great joy . . . blessing God . . .'

To return, in this way, twenty-two times in twenty-four chapters, to the effect of the coming of Jesus among men as joy, gladness, praise, and thanksgiving, leaves no doubt of the way Luke conceived the difference Jesus made to men's experience. Christianity was doing far more for people in that bemused, decaying, disintegrating society than any Mystery-cult, philosophy or political revolution could do. Life gained meaning, value, zest and purpose in Jesus, far outweighing the cost of Christian discipline and self-denial.

If Luke's contribution to the New Testament had been better appreciated, the church might have been spared the more extreme forms of asceticism which imagined some Christian virtue in the cult of dirt, hunger, vermin, flagellation, indignity, masochism, and other useless, negative, impoverishing, and life-debasing practices which Christian devotion adopted in later years. It would be difficult indeed to place Simon Stylites, unkempt, dirty, evil-smelling, emaciated, and more than half mad, after forty years alone on his pillar in the desert — or any of his fellow 'saints', walled up for years, living down wells, wallowing in marshes, going on all fours, self-loathing and self-torturing — among Luke's gallery of the lives transformed, irradiated, enriched, *made healthy*, by Christ.

The eastern churches, making John their pre-eminent New Testament teacher, and the central gift of the gospel eternal life through Christ's incarnation and resurrection, retained more of the Lukan emphasis on the positive value of salvation, though perhaps thinking more of the next world than of this. The western churches, idolizing Paul, whose unavoidable controversies with Judaism and gnosticism concentrated more upon atonement for guilt, escaping condemnation, and subduing the flesh, have tended to sound far more doctrinal, negative, repressive, and forbidding. Luke, who after all wrote more of the New Testament than either Paul or John, could teach the modern church of east and west, north and south, to expect from Christ, here and now, an invigorating, liberating, joyous, life-enhancing zest and drive, that would make the world again envy the Christian lifestyle, and enquire its explanation.

The Social Task

One curious change of emphasis distinguishes Luke's two volumes, and serves to draw attention to the way in which Luke thinks of the Christian movement and its function in the world. In the Gospel, Luke never mentions 'the church', but refers to the 'kingdom' thirty-eight times. As we have seen, in Luke's thought the kingdom of God is the experience, which the Father is pleased to 'give' us, of life under divine rule, exemplified in Jesus. The kingdom *has* come in those who so live, and so is already 'among us'. It ferments and grows within society like leaven and seed; men 'enter' it, by repentance and childlike acceptance, though some find it 'hard' to do so. In its full consummation and power the kingdom is still to come, and men wait for, pray for, and seek it. God's agent in establishing it is Jesus, who gathers round him disciples who share in the experience, the vision, and the task of proclaiming the kingdom and sharing its blessings with the surrounding world. That circle around Jesus is the nearest approach in the Gospel to the 'church'.

In Luke's second volume, the kingdom is mentioned rarely, six times as the subject of Christian evangelism and teaching, once as a (mistaken) hope of restoration to Israel (1:6), and once as entered only through tribulation. The overwhelming emphasis in *Acts* falls upon the church, mentioned nineteen times (the *word* is also used of Israel in the wilderness, and of the town-meeting at Ephesus, 19:41 Greek), and described in detail throughout the book. It is this church, the extended circle of disciples with the risen Jesus still in their midst by his Spirit, which is now God's agent in establishing the kingdom. In its own surrendered and guided life, the church shows what the reign of God means; in its transformed membership it shows what the reign of God can do for individuals; and in its ministry of word and power to the world around, it shows what the reign of God could accomplish in society.

For, as in the Gospel so in *Acts*, the kingdom of God reaches out through those who already enjoy its blessings to bless and enrich the lives around it. In and through the church, the kingdom has come and is coming to many, and will yet come in power in the world.

This emphasis upon the church could be seriously misleading unless we recall that nothing remotely resembling an institution, a hierarchy, a well-organized and homogenous 'society', is in Luke's mind. Most frequently in Acts the word means simply the local congregation of Christians in any one place, or the total of such congregations in any district (the church at Jerusalem, Antioch, Ephesus, the churches in Judea — sixteen times out of the nineteen Christian applications of the word). This may be its meaning also in the other three places (15:22, 8:3, 12:1), though these may carry some slight sense of 'the church as a whole, wherever it is to be found, the universal church of Christ'. What Luke thus means by 'the church' is a scattering of diverse and separated congregations, or fellowships, of believers in Christ, recognizing each other, creating new groups, but in no other way as yet united in discipline or government. The chief links between them were the shared faith and sacraments, and travelling apostles, evangelists and pastors. In forms of worship and rudimentary organization the congregations differed widely from each other. These individuals-in-groups were the new and multiplying 'disciples', who were agents of the kingdom they preached and sought. Luke estimates that some weeks after Pentecost there were about five thousand men within the Jerusalem church (4:4) — a thousand less than the sect of the Pharisees.

This is the church that was for Luke the vehicle of the present reign of God in the world, and of the coming kingdom of power and glory.

That hope of the kingdom's ultimate triumph appears to take first place in Luke's thought of the church's future. As in the Gospel he had preserved older eschatological images of the return of Christ (21:25–38), so in *Acts* he preserves the promise that 'this same Jesus shall so come . . .' (1:10–11, compare 17:31, 3:19–21). But if Luke makes less than Mark, or Matthew, of the imminence of the Advent, it is only because he is so vividly aware of the presence of Christ in power, already, within the church he knows, and of the advance of the kingdom through the church's work and witness. Luke is informing Theophilus of things which *'have been* accomplished among us' (Luke 1:1). Without obscuring a final fulfilment when the Son of man will come (Luke 21:27), Luke emphasizes what is being fulfilled, daily, over wider and wider areas of the world, in the activity of Christ within the church (Acts 1:1).

That activity was especially a ministry of truth and grace towards the broken and sinful — as it had been during the days of his visible presence; towards people of all lands and races; towards rival groups and nations, preaching reconciliation and peace; towards the sick and the afflicted, offering comfort and healing; towards women undervalued or degraded, offering dignity and cleansing; and towards the poor and disadvantaged, offering generosity and compassion. In Christ's name the church preached a kingdom of human values, its origin and resources unmistakably divine. In all these ways Christ's 'earthly' ministry continued within society, God's kingdom drew nearer, and the presence of Christ was demonstrated in the attitude of the church towards the rest of society, as his Spirit directed, energized, sustained, and extended, the number of those who were being saved.

Out of all proportion to its size, and in spite of its political naivety, the church possessed an inner strength to expand, courage to resist, readiness to suffer, and resources to survive and to serve, that made it just such a force for social welfare, constructive concern, and creative idealism, as that ancient world sorely needed. In the second century, the sheer goodness of Christians in caring for the plague-ridden, for unwanted children, for slaves, the old, the helpless, and prisoners of war, for lepers and the condemned, and for all who were handicapped or sick or dying, earned the outspoken admiration of pagan leaders. The 'superstitious beliefs' of Christians were still despised, but for a few decades pagans were urged to emulate Christians in their social concern and selflessness. The phenomenal spread of Christianity through the Roman world was attributed by one writer to the reputation that Christians bore, wherever they were met, as 'good to know'.

The church at that time was fulfilling nobly Luke's positive conception of her social task, to serve men and women everywhere, in the name of the Friend of all in need of friendship. Then came the long period of withdrawal, antagonism, and rejection. The world came to be seen as the realm of Satan. Persecution and corruption combined to drive the church into monastic escape from the world, seeking security; later, into mystic retreat from the world, seeking a spirituality unrelated to the problems of other men; and later still, into Puritan separation from the world seeking a sanctification uncontaminated by the world. Christians who found these attitudes unrewarding tended to take advantage of the nominal conversion of the Roman empire to seek to dominate the world; or, when Europe broke into separate small States, to exercise spiritual authority over governments (as at Geneva) in the name of God's 'sovereignty'.

Of course there were exceptions, socially useful monasteries whose monks brought charity and instruction into the lives of hardpressed peasants, and evangelical organizations of many kinds which sought to alleviate society's worst ills. *If Luke's contribution to the New Testament had been better appreciated*, the church might have been spared years of social irrelevance, and of bitter criticism, as concerned only with the rich and powerful, and more anxious about her own privileges and freedoms than about the hunger and distress around her.

Not until the church rediscovered the Lukan conception of the kingdom of God in the mid-nineteenth century did she return, even in part, and slowly, to the positive, joyous, socially relevant and creative, life-enhancing and world-enriching gospel which Luke expounded to Theophilus. And to the portrait of the strong, compassionate, human Christ, who invaded history with divine power to share man's suffering, serve man's need, and save both individuals and society.

Until the church presents again, to a divided, bewildered, and frightened world, such an image of Christ, such a demonstration of ample power channelled through compassion into redemptive service, there will be no reason why men should admire, or envy, the Christian lifestyle, seek its explanation, or listen with respect to Luke's case for Christianity.

INDEX

111